SEASONS

of the

UNKNOWN

FROM BATHROOM FLOOR TO GOD'S PURPOSE

DWAYNE LIVERMORE

Paperback ISBN: 979-8-89741-047-7
eBook ISBN: 979-8-89741-048-4

Editing and design by **The 1 and Only Publishing**

Published by
The 1 and Only Publishing
4500 Forbes Blvd
Lanham, MD 20706
info@the1andonlypublishing.com
www.the1andonlypublishing.com

Printed in the United States of America
First Edition

To God—
thank You for placing this vision within me
and giving me the strength to see it through.
In every moment of doubt and weariness,
You carried me.
This is for Your purpose, not mine.
And to every reader—
may this be a reminder that what you're facing
is only a season.
It will not last forever—
this season will pass.

Contents

THE SEASONS BEGIN

I STILL REMEMBER THE NIGHTS ON THE COLD BATHROOM FLOOR. Cardboard boxes beneath my body—flattened, worn, barely softening the concrete that pressed against my bones. The bathroom wasn't finished. Just raw concrete walls, piles of dirty clothes in the corners, and me. A child curled up, alone, in a space that smelled of mildew and neglect. Insects crawled over me in the darkness. By morning, my skin would be swollen with bites. My body ached. I was sick most of the time.

Everyone else in the house had a bed. Everyone else had warmth, a pillow, a blanket. But not me.

I was different. And in my world, *different* meant *unwanted*.

That bathroom floor is more than a memory—it's a symbol. It represents the starting point of a journey I never asked for but couldn't escape. A journey marked by pain, survival, and somehow, against all logic, the relentless presence of a God. I couldn't always see Him, but He was there, and He refused to let me go.

Growing up in Jamaica, I knew chaos before I knew peace. I knew verbal abuse before I knew encouragement. I knew hunger before I knew provision. My mother, battling her own demons, could not love me the way a child needs to be loved. My father was absent. The community around me was quick to judge, to label, to mock.

Words like "Battyman" and "You fi dead" became the soundtrack of my childhood. I never heard, "I'm proud of you" or "You're doing well." Instead, I was sent out at midnight to fetch alcohol and weed for my mother—a child walking dark roads where anything could happen, praying under my breath that I'd make it home.

And yet—I survived.

Not because of my own strength. Not because I had resources or support or a safety net. I survived because of God. Even when I couldn't articulate it, even when I was too young to understand theology or doctrine, I felt His covering. He placed people in my life for certain seasons—some stayed only briefly, others lingered longer—but each one was part of a divine orchestration I'm only now beginning to fully understand.

THE FOUR SEASONS OF TRANSFORMATION

This book is not just my story. It's a testimony of how God takes the broken pieces of a life—rejection, abuse, shame, hunger, betrayal—and uses every single fragment to build something with purpose. My life has moved in distinct seasons, painful but necessary stages that I've come to recognize as God's process of refining me:

1. REMOVING

God begins by pulling away what was never meant to stay. Toxic relationships. Destructive patterns. People who were assigned to a moment, not a lifetime. This season feels like loss, but it's actually protection. You can't carry new wine in old wineskins. God has to remove the old to make room for what He's preparing.

2. SEPARATING

Separation is one of the loneliest seasons. You're set apart—often painfully—from everything familiar. Friends drift away. Opportunities close. You find yourself isolated, questioning if you did something wrong. But separation isn't punishment—it's preparation. God separates you so He can speak to you clearly, without the noise of other voices drowning out His direction.

3. PREPARING

This is the season of the fire. The refining. The shaping. It's where your character is tested, your faith is stretched, and your endurance is built. You're being equipped for something bigger than you can see in the moment. Preparation doesn't feel productive—it feels repetitive, exhausting, sometimes pointless. But every trial is part of His curriculum. Every hardship is sharpening you for the assignment ahead.

4. RELEASING

Finally, God releases you into your purpose. What you endured, what you learned, what you overcame—it all positions you to step boldly into your calling. The release isn't the end of struggle, but rather, accepting your authority and the anointing you've been prepared for. This is when your testimony becomes a tool to set others free.

WHY I'M WRITING THIS

You may see your own life in these pages. You may be in the middle of one of these seasons right now—feeling removed, separated, prepared, or on the edge of release. If so, I pray my testimony reminds you of this truth: **God has not left you. Even in the bathroom floor moments, He sees you.**

There were nights when I wanted to die. Mornings when I couldn't imagine surviving another day of ridicule, another beating, another hungry walk to school. The weight of raising my four younger siblings when I was just a child myself.

The shame of wetting the bed into my teenage years because my body had been damaged by the strain of doing adult labor as a boy. The terror of being robbed at gunpoint weeks before moving to America for graduate school. The betrayal of people I trusted—family, friends, even church members—who spoke one thing to my face and another behind my back.

But I'm still here.

At 27 years old, I stand as proof that what the enemy means for evil, God will turn for good. I stand as proof that generational curses can be broken. That childhood trauma doesn't have to define your destiny. That even when you're labeled, mocked, abused, and abandoned, God is still writing your story—and the ending is redemption.

THIS BOOK IS FOR YOU IF:

- You've been abused—verbally, physically, emotionally—and you're wondering if healing is even possible.
- You've been rejected because you're "different," and the world has tried to convince you that *different* means *broken*.
- You've been betrayed by people who were supposed to protect you.
- You've battled suicidal thoughts, depression, and the quiet war that wages in your mind when no one else can see.
- You've gone without—without food, without money, without love—and you're tired of just surviving.
- You're in a season that makes no sense, You feel empty inside, spiritually low and are experiencing heavy warfare.
- You want to understand. Maybe you've never experienced severe trauma, but you love someone who has. Maybe you're a pastor, counselor, teacher, or friend who wants to know how to walk alongside the broken without offering shallow platitudes. My story can help you see what survival really looks like—and what true healing requires.

A NOTE BEFORE WE BEGIN

I'm not a perfect person. I've made mistakes. I've sinned. I've been disobedient when God called me higher. There were seasons when I walked away from the church because the people in it hurt me deeply. There were moments when I sought love in places and people I shouldn't have. I've stumbled, fallen, and had to get back up more times than I can count.

But that's the point.

This isn't a book about perfection. It's a book about process. It's about a God who doesn't give up on you even when you've given up on yourself. It's about the seasons we all go through—the ones we can't skip, can't rush, and can't avoid—that shape us into who we're meant to become.

So if you're expecting a sanitized, Instagram-perfect testimony, this isn't it. What you'll find here is raw. Real. Unfiltered. There are parts of my story I'm still healing from. There are wounds that still ache when I press on them. But I believe in the power of truth-telling. I believe that when we're honest about our pain, we give others permission to be honest about theirs. And in that honesty, healing begins.

LET'S WALK TOGETHER

As you read, I encourage you to pause. Reflect. Let the Holy Spirit speak to you. At the end of each chapter, you'll find a reflection prompt—a question designed to help you process your own seasons, your own pain, your own purpose.

This isn't just my story. It's an invitation into yours.

So take a breath. Say a prayer. And let's begin.

CHAPTER 1

THE GIFT IN DIFFERENCE

I REMEMBER KINDERGARTEN LIKE IT WAS YESTERDAY.
The world was supposed to feel simple at that age. Safe. Full of crayons and snack time and making friends on the playground. But even then—at five, maybe six years old—I knew something that no child should have to recognize so early: Something about me didn't fit.

It wasn't something I chose. It wasn't something I could hide, no matter how hard I tried. It was just there, woven into the fabric of who I was. The way I walked. The way I talked. The way I carried myself with a quietness, a gentleness, a sensitivity that the other boys didn't have. I was more thoughtful. More careful with my words. More in tune with feelings and emotions that others seemed to brush past without noticing.

I didn't play rough like the other boys. I wasn't interested in football, wasn't drawn to the loud, aggressive games that seemed to define masculinity in my community. I found myself gravitating toward the girls—I felt safer there. I felt seen. They weren't trying to prove anything. They weren't trying to dominate or intimidate. They just *were*, and I wanted to just *be* too.

But the world didn't let me.

LABELED BEFORE I COULD DEFINE MYSELF

By the time I was in primary school, the whispers had already started. Teachers looked at me sideways. Classmates snickered behind cupped hands. Even strangers—adults who didn't know my name—felt entitled to pass judgment on a child they'd only seen in passing.

"Battyman."

That word became my shadow. In Jamaica, it's one of the worst things you can be called. It's not just an insult—it's a death sentence in some circles. It's a word that marks you, isolates you, and makes you a target. And they threw it at me before I even understood what it meant.

I didn't know why I stood out. I didn't wake up one day and decide to be polished. I just was. And for that—for simply existing in a body and spirit that didn't conform to what others expected—I was branded. Mocked. Feared. Hated.

The boys at school were merciless. They called me names. They pushed me in the hallways. They made sure I knew I didn't belong. Even when I tried to keep my head down, to stay quiet, to make myself invisible, they found me. They *always* found me.

And it wasn't just the boys. Grown men in my community—men who should have been protectors, examples, guides—looked at me with disgust. They laughed. They made jokes. They said things within earshot that no child should hear about themself. I was a punchline before I'd even learned to read properly.

But the deepest wound—the one that cut straight to my soul—came from home.

WHEN YOUR OWN MOTHER SPEAKS THE CURSE

My mother didn't protect me. She didn't defend me. She didn't pull me aside and tell me that I was fearfully and wonderfully made, that God had a plan for my life, or that the opinions of others didn't define my worth.

She was one of the first to call me "Battyman," and many other names.

I'll never forget the way her face twisted when she looked at me. The way her voice dripped with contempt. She cursed me. She told me I was disgusting. She told me I would never amount to anything. She said I was worthless, that I should have never been born, that the world would be better off without me, and that I should go look for my deadbeat father.

Imagine hearing that from the woman who gave you life. Imagine being a child—small, vulnerable, desperate for love—and being told by your own mother that you're a mistake.

I cried. God, I cried so much. In secret, where no one could see. Because even my tears felt like proof that I was weak, that I was everything they said I was. I learned early to swallow my pain, to hide my hurt, to keep moving even when every part of me wanted to collapse.

There were days I didn't want to go to school because I knew what awaited me. Days I prayed to wake up and be someone else—anyone else. Days I stared at my reflection and wondered what was so wrong with me that even my own family couldn't love me.

But in those dark moments, something else was happening too. Something I couldn't see at the time but can recognize now, looking back.

God was laying a foundation in me—one not built on people's approval, but on something far more lasting. I learned that God allowed them to trample upon my character because he wanted to remove me from the place I was, not just the physical location, but the spiritual location, so I could learn who he is. This is how God works sometimes, he uses anything in life to get you to know and understand who he truly is for yourself.

THE COST OF STANDING OUT

I won't sugarcoat this: Being set apart comes with a cost. People will misunderstand you. They'll project their fears, their insecurities, their biases onto you. They'll try to shrink you down to a size that makes them comfortable. They'll ask you to dim your light so they don't have to confront their own darkness.

And sometimes, that rejection will come from the people closest to you. Family. Friends. The church. The very places that should be safe will become battlegrounds.

That pain is real. I'm not going to tell you to just "get over it" or "forgive and forget." Wounds like that leave scars. They change you. They make you cautious, guarded, and slower to trust.

The isolation was suffocating. I felt like I was drowning in a sea of people who all seemed to speak the same language—a language I didn't understand and couldn't learn. They moved through the world with ease, with belonging, while I stumbled through each day, wondering if there would ever be a place for someone like me.

I started to believe the narrative they fed me: that something was fundamentally wrong with me. That I was broken beyond repair. That the best I could hope for was to survive, not to thrive.

But even then, even in my deepest moments of self-doubt, there was a quiet voice—faint but persistent—whispering that there was more to my story than what they were telling me.

WHEN REJECTION BECOMES PREPARATION

Here's what I've learned over the years, through all the pain and confusion and rejection: What the world calls "different," God calls "set apart."

The world wants everyone to fit into neat, predictable boxes. But God doesn't operate that way. He creates originals, not copies. And when He places something distinct in you—something that sets you apart, something that makes you think differently, feel differently, move differently—it's not an accident. It's intentional.

I was being prepared.

Every insult, every mocking glance, every whisper behind my back was shaping me. It was teaching me resilience. It was teaching me empathy. It was teaching me to lean not on the approval of people, but on the acceptance of God.

Looking back now, I can see the curriculum hidden in the chaos. Each rejection taught me discernment—how to recognize who was safe and who wasn't. Each moment of isolation taught me to find comfort in God's presence when human companionship failed. Each harsh word directed at me made me more careful with my own, more aware of their power to build up or tear down.

The Apostle Paul wrote in Ephesians 2:10, *"For we are God's handiwork, created in Christ Jesus to do good works, which God prepared in advance for us to do."*

That word, "handiwork," stopped me in my tracks when I first really read it as a teenager. It's not just "creation"—it's craftsmanship. It's art. It's something made with intention, care, and purpose.

I am God's handiwork. Not a mistake. Not an accident. Not a cosmic error that slipped through the cracks. I was created intentionally, with purpose, for a specific calling that required me to be exactly who I am.

THE GIFT HIDDEN IN THE STRUGGLE

The same is true for you.

If you've ever felt out of place—if you've ever been the odd one out, the one who didn't fit, the one others didn't understand—I want you to know something: That distinction is your gift. It's what will allow you to reach people others can't reach. It's what will give you insight others don't have. It's what will make your testimony powerful.

The enemy wants you to believe that being set apart makes you defective. That's a lie. The truth is, being set apart makes you *dangerous* to the kingdom of darkness. Because when you walk in the fullness of who God created you to be—not who others told you to be—you become unstoppable.

Looking back now, I can see how my sensitivity became my strength.

Because I felt deeply, I learned to read people. I learned to see the pain others tried to hide. I learned to offer compassion to the overlooked and the outcast—because I knew what it felt like to be both.

Because I was rejected, I learned to depend on God in ways I never would have if life had been easy. My relationship with Him became real, raw, necessary—not just Sunday morning religion, but daily survival.

Because I was misunderstood, I learned to trust God's voice over the noise of the crowd. I learned to seek His validation instead of chasing approval from people who would never truly see me.

My difference didn't disqualify me. It *qualified* me for the work God has called me to do.

FINDING IDENTITY BEYOND THE LABELS

It took me years—decades, really—to stop letting other people's labels define me. To stop internalizing the lies. To stop believing that the names they called me were who I actually was.

Even now, at 27, I'm still unlearning some of those messages. Still peeling back layers of shame. Still learning to see myself the way God sees me.

But here's what I know for sure: My identity is not found in what people say about me. It's found in what God says about me.

He says I am loved. Chosen. Redeemed. Set apart. Equipped. Called. Anointed.

He says I am His masterpiece, His workmanship, crafted with intention and care.

He says the plans He has for me are good—plans to give me hope and a future, plans for me to prosper.

Those are the truths I cling to now. Not the taunts of bullies. Not the curses of my mother. Not the judgment of strangers who never took the time to know my heart.

If you're reading this and you've been labeled, branded, written off—hear me: You are more than what they say about you. You are more than the worst thing anyone has ever called you. You are a child of the Most High God, created in His image, filled with His breath, destined for His glory.

Don't let anyone—*anyone*—convince you otherwise.

As I write this now, I feel the weight of those words in a way I couldn't as a child. Back then, I was just trying to survive. Now, I can see the architecture of God's plan—how every piece of my pain was building toward something purposeful. That doesn't make what I endured right or acceptable. But it does mean God wasted nothing.

THE BRIDGE FORWARD

Understanding that I was created with purpose was the first step. But knowing something intellectually and feeling it in your bones are two different things. The labels others put on me had done more than hurt my feelings—they had wounded my soul, shaped how I saw myself, and infected the way I moved through the world.

And those labels? They didn't just come from strangers and schoolmates. The deepest cuts came from the words spoken inside my own home, from the mouth of the woman who should have been my first defender.

Words, I would learn, have power. And the wounds they create can last far longer than any physical scar.

SCRIPTURE ANCHOR

"For we are God's handiwork, created in Christ Jesus to do good works, which God prepared in advance for us to do."

— EPHESIANS 2:10 (NIV)

KEY LESSON

Being set apart is not a flaw—it's a sign of divine assignment. Early feelings of isolation or misunderstanding cultivate resilience, perspective, and spiritual strength. Your individuality is a gift, and anchoring your identity in God's truth transforms what once felt like weakness into a foundation for destiny.

REFLECTION MOMENT

Pause here and consider: When have you felt "different" or misunderstood in your life? How did that experience shape you? In what ways might God have been using that distinction to prepare you for something only you could do?

Write down one way you can begin to see your uniqueness as a gift rather than a burden.

CHAPTER 2

WORDS THAT WOUND

Words have power.

They can build up or tear down. They can breathe life into a dying soul, or suck the breath right out of someone who's already suffocating. They can heal wounds you can't see, or create scars that never fully fade.

Growing up, words were weapons in my house. Sharp. Intentional. Designed to cut deep and leave lasting damage. And the person wielding those weapons most often wasn't a stranger or a bully at school—it was my mother.

The woman who gave me life became the woman who tried to destroy it with her words.

THE FIRST VOICE THAT BROKE ME

Children are supposed to hear certain things from their mothers. "I love you." "I'm proud of you." "You're going to do great things." Those words are supposed to lay a foundation—a sense of worth, of belonging, of safety.

I never heard those words.

Instead, I heard: "Mi hate yuh." "Yuh disgusting." "Yuh fi dead." "Yuh sick mi."

She said these things with such venom, such conviction, that, even as a child, I believed her. Why wouldn't I? She was my mother. If she couldn't love me, if she couldn't see anything good in me, then maybe there really was nothing good to see.

The abuse started early.

I was still in primary school—maybe eight or nine years old—when it became clear that I occupied a different space in her world than my siblings did. They weren't treated the way I was. They weren't cursed at with the same frequency or intensity. They didn't carry the weight of her anger, her disappointment, her rage the way I did.

I was the target. The scapegoat. The one she took everything out on. And it wasn't just the words themselves—it was the *way* she said them: with her whole chest. Like she meant every syllable. Like she wanted to make sure I felt them, that they sank in deep, that they took root in my soul and poisoned everything good I might have believed about myself.

You would think she was cursing one of her enemies, not her own child.

I prayed every day to become 18 or older, so I could leave.

I remember one particular evening—I couldn't have been more than ten—when she went on a rampage. I don't even remember what triggered it. Maybe I'd done something wrong, or maybe I'd simply existed in a way that irritated her. But she tore into me with words that felt like physical blows.

She told me, That she wished she'd never had me. That my very existence was a burden she shouldn't have to carry.

I stood there, frozen, tears streaming down my face, trying to make myself smaller, trying to disappear into the walls. My siblings watched from the doorway, silent, afraid to intervene. They'd learned early that stepping between her and her target only shifted the rage onto them.

When she finally finished, she dismissed me with a wave of her hand, like I was nothing. Like I didn't matter. Like my tears, my pain, and my breaking heart were just noise she didn't want to hear.

I went outside and sat under a tree in the yard. The sun was setting, painting the sky in shades of orange and pink—beautiful, indifferent to my suffering. And I remember thinking, *Is this what my whole life is going to be? Is this all I'm worth?*

Now, looking back, I can see that moment as a crossroads. I could have let her words become my truth. I could have let them define the trajectory of my life. And for a long time, I did. But somewhere deep inside, a small voice was already whispering that her words weren't the final authority on my life.

MIDNIGHT MISSIONS AND MANUFACTURED SHAME

The verbal abuse was constant, but it wasn't the only way she showed me I didn't matter.

She would send me out late at night—sometimes as late as midnight—to go beg her friends for weed, alcohol, money or whatever she needed to feed her addictions.

I was just a child. I didn't know how to say no. I didn't know I *could* say no.

So I went.

I walked those dark roads alone, scared, crying, praying I wouldn't get hurt. Jamaica at night is not safe for a grown man, let alone a small boy. I didn't know who was out there. I didn't know if someone would attack me, kidnap me, or worse.

My mother didn't care. My safety wasn't her concern. Her next drink was.

I remember the shame I felt, knocking on doors at that hour, asking adults for things no child should even know about. Some of them looked at me with pity. Others looked annoyed. A few refused and sent me away empty-handed, which meant I'd have to return home and face her wrath.

One night I went to the shop to buy a pack of cigarettes. A man standing nearby looked at me, then at the box, and asked me to read what was written on it.

I struggled through the words, barely able to pronounce them.

"Keep out of reach of minors."

He paused, then looked back at me.

"You know you shouldn't be buying this, right?"

I didn't answer him.

Because in my mind, I was thinking, *you don't know my mother.*

If you did, you wouldn't be saying anything at all.

The worst part wasn't even the danger or the embarrassment or even failing to convince her that those people refused to help. It was the message those errands sent: *You are disposable. Your safety, your dignity, your childhood—none of it matters.*

Even as a young boy, I knew this wasn't normal. I knew other kids weren't living like this. But I also didn't know what to do about it. There was no one to tell. No one to run to. So I endured.

And with every trip, with every degrading errand, the message became clearer: *You don't matter. Your life has no value.*

WORDS FROM THE COMMUNITY

It wasn't just my mother. The community I grew up in was ruthless, too.

Every insult was a brick. Every joke at my expense was a stone. And slowly, those bricks and stones built a wall around my heart—thick, heavy, suffocating. And when you're a child who hears those messages over and over from the people who are supposed to love you, the community that's supposed to protect you, you start to lose sight of who you really are.

One day, I was walking home from school, and a group of older boys started following me, chanting slurs. I walked faster. So did they. I started running, my backpack bouncing against my spine, my heart hammering in my chest.

They didn't catch me that day. But the fear stayed with me. The knowledge that the world saw me as prey.

I learned to make myself small. To move quietly. To avoid eye contact. To become invisible when I could, and endure when I couldn't. These weren't survival skills I chose—they were forced upon me by a world determined to remind me I didn't belong.

THE INTERNAL ECHO CHAMBER

The words echoed in my mind long after they were spoken. I'd lie awake at night, replaying them. My mother's voice. The laughter of my peers. The disgust in the eyes of adults who should have known better. And those replays became my internal dialogue.

You're not good enough.

No one will ever love you.

You're disgusting.

You should just die.

I started to believe that maybe the world would be better off without me. Maybe I was the problem. That maybe if I just disappeared, everyone else's life would be easier.

That's what verbal abuse does. It doesn't just hurt in the moment—it plants seeds. Seeds of shame, self-hatred, and despair. And if you're not careful, those seeds grow into something much darker.

There were times I wanted to end it all. Times I thought about ways to make the pain stop.

But something kept me here. Something I couldn't fully explain at the time, but now recognize as God's hand holding me, even when I couldn't feel it.

I believe now that God sends angels to people on the brink. Not always literal angels, but moments—small, seemingly insignificant moments—that interrupt the spiral. A bird that suddenly appeared and distracted me. A neighbor who called my name just as I was about to do something irreversible. A memory of my grandmother's prayers that flooded my mind at exactly the right time.

These weren't coincidences. They were divine interventions.

THE POWER OF THE TONGUE

Proverbs 18:21 says, *"The tongue has the power of life and death, and those who love it will eat its fruit."*

That scripture became deeply personal to me, because I lived it. I saw, firsthand, how words could kill a person's spirit, even if their body kept moving. But I also came to understand something powerful: Just because someone speaks death over you doesn't mean you have to accept it.

Words have power, yes. But they don't have the *final* say. God's Word has the final say. And what He says about me is infinitely more true, more lasting, more powerful than anything anyone else could ever speak over my life.

It took me years to get to that place. Years of unlearning the lies. Years of replacing the negative voices with God's devotion. Years of standing in front of the mirror and speaking life over myself, even when I didn't fully believe in it yet.

I started small. I'd whisper scriptures to myself in the bathroom, the only place I had privacy. *"I am fearfully and wonderfully made."* At first, the words felt empty, like I was lying to myself.

But I kept saying them anyway.

"I am loved."

"I have a future."

"God has a plan for my life."

Slowly—painfully slowly—those death-filled words started losing their grip.

Healing from verbal abuse isn't a single moment. It's not a prayer you speak once, and everything changes. It's a daily, sometimes hourly, decision to reject lies and embrace the truth. It's choosing God's voice over the chorus of those who have spoken death over you.

And some days, you'll lose that battle. Some days, the old voices will be louder. But even on those days, you keep fighting. Because every time you choose truth over lies, you're rewriting the script. You're taking back the power those words once had over you.

LEARNING TO GUARD MY HEART

Proverbs 4:23 says, *"Above all else, guard your heart, for everything you do flows from it."*

I didn't know how to do that as a child. I let everyone's words in. I absorbed them, internalized them, and made them my identity. But as I got older and began to heal, I realized I had a choice. I could either keep letting other people's opinions define me, or I could build boundaries around my heart and only let in voices that aligned with God's truth.

That doesn't mean I became hard or closed off. It means I became discerning. I learned to recognize which voices were speaking life and which were speaking death. I learned to reject the ones that didn't line up with who God said I was.

And that shift—that decision to guard my heart and filter what I allowed in—changed everything.

I started asking myself questions before I let words sink in:

- Does this align with what God says about me?

- Is this person speaking from a place of love, or from their own brokenness?
- Will believing these words move me closer to God's purpose, or further from it?

These questions became my filter. My protection.

WORDS CAN ALSO HEAL

Here's the other side of the coin: Just as words can wound, they can also heal.

God's Word became my refuge. When the world told me I was worthless, Scripture told me I was fearfully and wonderfully made. When people said I'd never amount to anything, God's Word said He had plans to prosper me. When shame tried to drown me, the Bible reminded me there was no condemnation for those who walk with Christ Jesus.

I also began to experience healing through the words of a few key people God placed in my life—people who spoke life over me when I needed it most. My grandmother. My great-grandmother. A teacher who saw potential in me. A mentor who believed in me when I didn't believe in myself.

Their words didn't erase the damage that had been done, but they planted new seeds. Seeds of hope, worth, and possibility. And over time, those seeds began to grow.

I remember one afternoon, sitting with my grandmother. I must have been about thirteen, in the thick of my worst years. I don't remember what prompted it, but she looked at me and said, "Dwayne, God has His hand on you. You're going to do great things. Don't let nobody tell you different."

It was such a simple statement. But it was the first time I remember someone speaking a blessing over my future instead of a curse. And I held onto those words like a lifeline.

Even now, when I'm struggling, when the old voices try to creep back in, I remember my grandmother's voice. I remember the certainty in her eyes. And I choose to believe her words over the ones that tried to destroy me.

BREAKING THE CYCLE

One of the most important decisions I've made is refusing to perpetuate the cycle of verbal abuse. I know what it's like to be on the receiving end of cruel words. I know how deeply they cut, how long they linger, how much damage they can do. And because I know that pain, I'm intentional about the words I speak over others.

I choose to encourage. To uplift. To speak life.

Does that mean I'm perfect? No. I've said things I regret. I've hurt people with my words, especially when I was younger and hadn't healed yet. Hurt people hurt people—that's the truth. But when I do cause harm, I apologize. I own it. I make it right.

Because I refuse to become the person who wounded me. I refuse to pass on the pain I received. The cycle ends with me.

I've made a commitment: I will not speak death. Not over myself, and not over others. I will use my words to build, not to destroy. To heal, not to wound. To speak the truth in love, not to tear down in anger.

This commitment has cost me. There have been times when I wanted to lash out, to hurt people the way I was hurt, to let my pain become their pain. But every time I've resisted that urge, every time I've chosen kindness over cruelty, I've felt a little more free.

Breaking cycles isn't easy. But it's necessary. And it's possible.

THE BRIDGE FORWARD

Understanding the power of words was crucial. But words weren't the only weapons used against me. There were places—physical spaces— where I was banished, isolated, made to feel like I was less than human.

24

One of those places was the cold bathroom floor, where I spent countless nights, exiled from the warmth and comfort the rest of my family enjoyed. It was there, in that forgotten space, that I learned what it truly meant to be alone—and what it meant to survive anyway.

SCRIPTURE ANCHOR

"The tongue has the power of life and death, and those who love it will eat its fruit."

— PROVERBS 18:21 (NIV)

"Above all else, guard your heart, for everything you do flows from it."

— PROVERBS 4:23 (NIV)

KEY LESSON

Words have the power to hurt, but they do not have the power to define you unless you allow them to. True identity and worth come from God, not from the opinions or cruelty of others. Learning to guard your heart and anchor your value in His truth transforms pain into strength. You also have the power to break cycles—to choose life-giving words and refuse to perpetuate the wounds you've received.

REFLECTION MOMENT

Take time to reflect: What words have wounded you most deeply? Are they still defining who you are today, or are you ready to let God's truth speak louder?

Write down one negative message you've believed about yourself, and beside it, write what God's Word says about you instead. Begin the practice of speaking that truth over yourself daily.

CHAPTER 3

THE FLOOR THAT RAISED ME

SOME NIGHTS, MY BEDROOM WASN'T A BEDROOM AT ALL. It was the cold, unfinished bathroom. Concrete floors. Piles of dirty laundry in the corners. No bed. No mattress. No comfort. Just me, a few flattened cardboard boxes, and whatever thin sheet I could find to lay over them.

That bathroom became my room—not because there wasn't space elsewhere in the house, but because my mother decided I didn't deserve to sleep where everyone else did.

I wet the bed. And for that, I was exiled.

THE SHAME THAT FOLLOWED ME

Bedwetting is something a lot of kids go through. It's common, treatable, and usually not something that lasts into the teenage years. But for me, it did.

It wasn't because I was lazy or careless. The doctor said something was wrong with my bladder—likely from all the heavy lifting I'd been doing from a young age. Washing clothes by hand for my siblings. Carrying water. Doing chores that should have been handled by adults, not a small boy whose body was still developing.

The strain damaged me. And one of the lasting effects was that I couldn't control my bladder at night.

My grandmother, who took me to the doctors, heard the explanation and told my mother. Although my mother knew this, she chose to ignore the issue. Because she didn't care. To her, my bedwetting was an inconvenience. A nuisance. Something that embarrassed her or made her life harder. So instead of getting me the help I needed, instead of showing compassion or patience, she punished me for it.

She made me sleep in the bathroom.

The shame was overwhelming. Not just the shame of wetting the bed—though that was bad enough—but the shame of being singled out, of being treated like I was dirty, like I was a problem that needed to be hidden away.

My siblings knew. The whole house knew. And no one said anything. No one stood up for me. No one questioned why a child was being forced to sleep on a concrete floor while everyone else had beds.

My father wasn't present.

I spoke to him on the phone sometimes, saw him a few times in person, but we never had a relationship. There was no real connection—no sense that he was invested in me or my life.

He knew, at least in part, what I was going through. Or maybe he knew just enough to know I wasn't okay. Still, he kept his distance. Maybe he believed I would be fine. Maybe it was easier for him to believe that.

He and my mother had a difficult relationship—tense, fractured in ways I didn't fully understand back then. I tell myself that's why he stayed away. That it wasn't about me.

The truth is, I don't even know if there was anything he could have done. I don't know if his presence would have changed anything at all.

But absence has its own weight.

I was invisible in my suffering.

Not unseen exactly—but unrecognized.

Reduced to an inconvenience. Something easier to overlook than to understand.

CARDBOARD AND CONCRETE: A CHILD'S BEDROOM

The bathroom was just a shell—four walls, a concrete floor, no fixtures, no tiles, nothing that made it usable. It was supposed to *become* a bathroom eventually, but at that point, it was just an empty, unfinished rooftop, cold space surrounded by piles of unwashed clothes.

That's where I slept. Every night. For years.

I'd gather cardboard boxes—whatever I could find from the market or the side of the road—and lay them flat on the floor. They were thin, flimsy, barely enough to create a barrier between my body and the hard ground beneath. Then I'd take a sheet, lay it over the cardboard, and curl up in a ball, trying to stay warm.

It was cold. So cold. The kind of cold that seeps into your bones and stays there, making you ache even after the sun comes up.

I got sick constantly. Respiratory infections. Colds that wouldn't go away. Fevers that left me shivering and weak. My body was always fighting something because I was sleeping in conditions no child should endure.

And the insects—God, the insects. Mosquitoes. Ants. Roaches, Centipedes (or Fortilegs, in Jamaica). Things that crawled over me in the dark, biting me, leaving my skin swollen and infected. I'd wake up scratching, covered in bites, my face puffy, my body hurting.

Some mornings, I'd look in the cracked mirror hanging on the wall and barely recognize myself.

But my mother didn't care.

Everyone else in the house had a bed. My siblings. My mother. Even her boyfriends who came and went. They all slept comfortably while I was banished to the bathroom floor, treated like I was less than human.

There was a night I lay there, listening to the sounds of the house—laughter from the other room, the television playing, normal life happening just a few feet away. And I felt so alone. So forgotten.

It was like I didn't exist.

I wonder, sometimes, how different my life might have been if some-one—anyone—had truly intervened. If a neighbor had pushed harder. If a teacher had noticed and asked questions. My grandmother lived with me and loved me deeply, but she was afraid- and sometimes, fear is its own kind of silence.

So I endured, night after night, year after year, invisible in my suffering.

THE NIGHTS I PRAYED

I prayed every night.

Not loud prayers. Not formal prayers. Just quiet, desperate pleas to a God I wasn't even sure was listening.

"Please, God, let me stop wetting the bed."

"Please, God, make this stop."

"Please, God, help me."

I didn't know how to pray eloquently. I didn't know the right words or the right scriptures. I just knew I needed help, and I didn't have any-one else to turn to.

So I prayed.

And I cried.

Every single night, I cried myself to sleep on that bathroom floor, feeling more alone than I ever thought possible. The darkness felt heavy, pressing down on me like a physical weight. The silence was deafening—broken only by the occasional sound of insects moving through the piles of clothes, or the drip of water from a pipe somewhere in the walls.

I'd pull that thin sheet over my head, creating a tiny cocoon, and whisper my prayers into the fabric. Sometimes, I'd pray for practical things—for the bedwetting to stop, for a real bed, for my mother to love me. Other times, I'd just pray to make it through the night.

But here's what I didn't understand at the time: **God was there.**

Even in that cold, dark, lonely space, He was with me. He saw me. He heard my prayers. And He was holding me together when everything in my life was trying to tear me apart.

Genesis 16:13 says, *"You are the God who sees me."* That's the God I was praying to, even though I didn't know it yet. The God who sees. The God who notices the forgotten, the rejected, the ones society throws away.

He saw me curled up on that bathroom floor. He counted every tear. He heard every whispered prayer. And though deliverance didn't come immediately—though I would spend years in that space—He was preparing something in me that could only be forged in that kind of darkness.

THE PHYSICAL TOLL

The conditions I lived in took a serious toll on my body.

I was sick more often than I was well. My immune system couldn't keep up with the constant exposure to cold, dampness, and unsanitary conditions. I missed school some days because I was too sick to go, or because my face was too swollen from insect bites to be seen in public.

My growth was stunted. I was smaller than other boys my age—thinner, weaker. The lack of proper sleep, nutrition, and living conditions all contributed to my body's struggle to develop normally.

But perhaps the most lasting damage was to my bladder. The doctor said the heavy lifting I'd been doing—lifting buckets of water, carrying loads of laundry, doing physical labor no child should be doing—had strained my muscles and damaged my bladder's function. The bedwetting wasn't just a phase I'd grow out of. It was a physical consequence of the life I was forced to live.

And yet, instead of addressing the root cause, instead of lightening my workload or getting me proper medical treatment, my mother punished me for the symptom.

It was a cruel irony: I was sleeping on that floor because of damage caused by the very work she forced me to do.

THE BREAKING POINT THAT DIDN'T BREAK ME

There came a point where I didn't think I could take it anymore.

I was maybe twelve or thirteen. I'd been sleeping on that bathroom floor for years by then. The novelty—if there ever was any—had long since worn off. What remained was just exhaustion. Physical exhaustion from never getting real rest. Emotional exhaustion from carrying shame and isolation every single day.

One night, after a particularly bad day—more verbal abuse from my mother, more mockery from my peers, more reminders that I was unwanted—I lay on that cardboard and genuinely wondered if I should just give up.

I thought about ways to end the pain. Ways to make it all stop. Ways to ensure I'd never have to face another morning of this life.

But something stopped me.

Maybe it was fear. Maybe it was that small spark of hope that refused to die no matter how much I tried to extinguish it. Maybe it was God Himself, speaking in that still, small voice, saying, *"Not yet. Hold on. There's more."*

I don't know what it was. But I held on. One more night. And then another. And another.

Looking back, I think that's one of the most powerful forms of faith: holding on when you can't see any reason to. When there's no evidence that things will get better. When every logical part of you says to quit. But you hold on anyway.

That's the faith that moves mountains. That's the faith that breaks generational curses. That's the faith that transforms victims into victors.

WHEN THE HEALING BEGAN

Eventually, I stopped wetting the bed. I don't remember exactly when it happened or what changed. Maybe it was the prayers finally being answered. Maybe it was my body finally healing from the strain. Maybe it was just time.

But one day, I woke up dry. And then another day. And another.

The relief was overwhelming. Not just because I was finally free from the physical problem, but because I thought—naively, hopefully— that maybe things would get better now. Maybe my mother would let me sleep inside with everyone else. Maybe I'd finally be treated like I belonged.

But that's not what happened.

Even after I stopped wetting the bed, I still slept in the bathroom for a while. The habit had been established. The message had been received. And my mother saw no reason to change the arrangement.

When I finally did move out of the bathroom, it wasn't because she decided I deserved better. It was because my great-grandmother intervened and took me in for a period of time. She gave me a place to sleep—sometimes, on the floor beside her bed, but at least it was carpeted, warmer, and I was with someone who genuinely cared about me.

But the damage was done. The message had been thoroughly

imprinted on my soul: *You are less than. You are Other. You are not worthy of the same love, care, and dignity that others receive.*

And that message stayed with me for years.

THE SCARS THAT REMAIN

I'd be lying if I said those nights on the bathroom floor don't still affect me.

Even now, at 27, I struggle with feelings of worthlessness. There are moments when that old voice creeps back in—the one that says I'm not enough, that I don't deserve good things, that I'm fundamentally broken.

I have dreams, sometimes, where I'm back in that bathroom. Cold. Alone. Forgotten. The cardboard beneath me, the insects crawling, the darkness pressing in.

And I wake up with my chest tight, my heart racing, tears on my face.

Trauma doesn't just disappear because you survived it. It leaves marks. It changes you. It shapes the way you see yourself and the world around you.

I still struggle with feeling like I'm a burden. When I'm in someone's home, I'm hyper-aware of taking up space, of being an inconvenience. I apologize too much. I make myself smaller than I need to be.

These are the lingering effects of being told, through words and actions, that my existence was a problem to be managed, rather than a gift to be celebrated.

Part of healing is acknowledging that those marks exist. It's not about pretending the trauma didn't happen or that it didn't affect you. It's about learning to live with the scars while refusing to let them define your future.

I'm still learning how to do that. Still learning how to be gentle with myself. Still learning that needing help, needing therapy, needing time to heal doesn't make me weak—it makes me human.

THE GIFT HIDDEN IN THE PAIN

Looking back now, I can see things I couldn't see then.

That bathroom floor taught me resilience. It taught me how to endure when everything in me wanted to give up. It taught me how to find God in the darkest, loneliest places. It also taught me compassion. Because I know what it feels like to be invisible, I see the invisible people now. The ones society overlooks. The ones struggling in silence. The ones sleeping on floors—literal or metaphorical—that no one else knows about.

My pain gave me eyes to see pain in others. My suffering gave me a heart for those who suffer.

And while I would never say I'm *grateful* for what I went through—because no child should endure that—I can say that God didn't waste it. He took that suffering and used it to shape me into someone who could help others who are suffering too.

That's not to justify what happened to me. Abuse is never okay. Neglect is never acceptable. What my mother did was wrong, and it left scars that I'm still healing from.

But God is a redeemer. He takes what was meant to destroy us, and transforms it into something that can be used for His glory and for the good of others.

Romans 8:28 says, *"And we know that in all things God works for the good of those who love him, who have been called according to his purpose."*

All things. *Even bathroom floors. Even cardboard beds. Even the nights you thought would never end. God was working. Even when I couldn't see it. Even when I felt abandoned, He was working.*

A WORD TO THOSE STILL ON THE FLOOR

If you're reading this and you're still in your "bathroom floor" season—whatever that looks like for you—I want you to know something:

You are not forgotten.

It might feel like no one sees you. Like no one cares. Like the world has written you off, decided you don't matter.

But God sees you. He knows exactly where you are and what you're going through. And He has not abandoned you.

The floor you're on right now—as cold and hard and unbearable as it feels—is not your final destination. It's just a chapter. A painful, difficult chapter, but still just a chapter. Hold on. Keep praying. Keep crying out to God. Keep believing that there's more for you than this moment.

Because there is.

I'm proof of that. I made it off that bathroom floor. I went from sleeping on cardboard to sleeping in my own apartment. I went from being told I'd never amount to anything to pursuing graduate degrees, currently doing my doctorate and writing books. I went from feeling worthless to understanding my worth in Christ.

If God could bring me through, He can bring you through, too.

Don't give up. Not tonight. Not tomorrow. Not ever. Your story isn't over. And the best chapters are still being written.

THE BRIDGE FORWARD

The bathroom floor taught me what it meant to be alone with my pain. But physical isolation wasn't the only wound I carried. There were other marks on my body—visible ones—that told a different story.

Bruises. Welts. Scars from objects turned into weapons.

Because the abuse I endured wasn't just emotional or verbal. It was physical. Violent. And it came from the same hands that should have held me, protected me, loved me.

The next chapter of my survival wasn't just about enduring neglect—it was about surviving blows that left marks on the outside and devastation on the inside.

SCRIPTURE ANCHOR

"You are the God who sees me."

— GENESIS 16:13 (NIV)

"And we know that in all things God works for the good of those who love him, who have been called according to his purpose."

— ROMANS 8:28 (NIV)

KEY LESSON

Even in the hidden and lonely moments, God sees you. The strength you build in those quiet struggles becomes the foundation for enduring life's hardest seasons. What feels like abandonment in the moment may be the very place where God is forging your resilience and preparing you for purpose. Never underestimate the power of holding on—even when holding on is all you can do.

REFLECTION MOMENT

Pause and consider: What are the "bathroom floor" moments in your life—the hidden struggles no one else knows about? How have those experiences shaped your strength and resilience? In what ways can you see God's presence now, even in places where you couldn't feel Him then?

Write down one thing you learned about yourself during a season of hidden suffering, and one way you can use that lesson to help someone else.

CHAPTER 4

BRUISES AND BETRAYAL

PHYSICAL ABUSE LEAVES MARKS THAT ARE BOTH VISIBLE AND invisible.

For me, the bruises were real—dark, swollen reminders of pain inflicted by the person who should have protected me the most: my mother. But the marks on my body were nothing compared to the wounds carved into my spirit.

Objects became weapons in her hands. A bat. A board. Stones. Bottles. Whatever was within reach when her rage boiled over became a tool of violence. And I—small, defenseless, desperate for love—became the target. I was a well-behaved child, but somehow, everything was a problem when it came to me.

The beatings weren't rare. They were regular. Expected. Part of the rhythm of my childhood. I learned to read the signs: the tightness in her jaw, the way her voice changed pitch, the heavy footsteps that meant I should make myself scarce. Even speaking up could earn me a beating- like the times she wore my clothes, the same ones I had spent all day washing while she was out at a bar, drinking and smoking.

I was not supposed to talk about her hypocrisy.

But there was nowhere to hide. Not really. The house wasn't big enough. And even when I tried to disappear, she always found me.

THE FIRST TIME I BLED

I don't remember what I did to provoke the first beating—if I even did anything at all. Maybe I spoke when I shouldn't have. Maybe I didn't move fast enough. Maybe I just existed in a way that reminded her of something she didn't want to see.

What I do remember is the board.

It was thick, heavy, rough. She swung it with her whole body, putting her weight behind it, and it connected with the side of my head. The impact was immediate—a white-hot flash of pain, a ringing in my ears that drowned out everything else.

I fell. The world tilted. And when I touched my head, my fingers came away wet and red.

Blood.

I remember staring at my hand, trying to make sense of what I was seeing.

I was bleeding.

My own mother had hit me so hard that I was bleeding.

I started to cry—not just from the pain, but from the shock, the betrayal, the crushing realization that this was my life. This was what love looked like in my house.

She didn't stop to check if I was okay. She didn't apologize. She didn't even pause. She just kept yelling, kept cursing, kept blaming me for whatever it was that had set her off in the first place.

I learned something that day: **Pain can come from the people who are supposed to love you most.**

WHEN YOUR BODY TELLS THE STORY

The beatings left marks. Not just bruises that faded after a few days, but deep, lasting evidence of violence.

My face would swell. My body would ache. Some mornings, I couldn't move without wincing. Other mornings, I couldn't go to school because the evidence was too visible—my face puffy, my skin discolored, my eyes bloodshot from crying.?

Insects from sleeping in the bathroom had left their marks too, but those bites were different from the bruises my mother left. The insect bites were accidental, thoughtless. The bruises from my mother were intentional.

She knew what she was doing. She aimed. She swung with purpose. She wanted me to feel it.

And I did.

Looking back now, I realize my body was telling a story I didn't have words for. The swelling, the bruises, the way I flinched when someone moved too quickly near me—all of it was testimony to a violence I was living through but couldn't articulate.

Children shouldn't have to carry their trauma on their skin. But I did. And the world saw it and looked away.

THE COMMUNITY THAT KNEW, BUT DID NOTHING

The beatings weren't a secret. They happened in a house with thin walls, in a community where sound traveled. People heard my cries. They heard her curses. They heard the sounds of objects hitting flesh, of a child screaming, of violence that should have been stopped.

And they knew.

My great-grandmother knew. My grandmother lived with us, witnessed much of it, but she was scared, too—scared of my mother's rage, scared of becoming the target herself. She tried to protect me when she could, but there were limits to what she could do.

The neighbors knew. Some of them even called Jamaica's child protective services—the CDA. They reported the abuse, told the agency what they'd heard and seen, and begged someone to intervene.

And the CDA came. Twice.

They showed up, asked questions, and looked around the house. But by the time they arrived, things were always calm. The evidence was hidden—or at least, not visible enough. My mother wasn't actively beating me when they knocked on the door. I wasn't crying in that moment. The house looked normal enough.

So they left. They said they'd keep monitoring the situation. They said they'd build a case. But they never came back.

And the neighbors? After the second time the CDA did nothing, they stopped calling. They became numb to the screaming, immune to the sounds of violence. They learned to turn up their radios when they heard me crying. They learned to look away when they saw my swollen face.

No one wanted to be the one to confront her. My mother had a reputation—she was known as the "Don of the Lane," a woman who carried herself like a man, who fought like a man, who didn't back down from anyone. People were afraid of her. Afraid of her temper. Afraid of becoming her target.

So they left me to survive on my own.

Betrayal doesn't always look like someone actively hurting you. Sometimes, it looks like people choosing to do nothing when they see you hurting. Sometimes, it's the silence of witnesses who could have spoken but didn't. Sometimes, it's systems that are supposed to protect children, but fail when it matters most.

I was betrayed not just by my mother's fists, but by a community that knew and did nothing. By neighbors who heard and turned away. By a system that investigated, but didn't intervene.

WHEN HELP CAME WITH STRINGS ATTACHED

There were a few people who tried to help. My grandmother did what she could within the limits of her fear. My great-grandmother, before she passed, offered me refuge when she could. And later, there was Mr. Murdoch—a man who saw my struggle and decided to step in.

Mr. Murdoch helped me in ways I'll always be grateful for. But even that help came with complications.

Over time, I started to feel like the help wasn't free. Like there were expectations attached to it. Like I owed something in return—not money, but obedience, loyalty, control over my decisions.

When I made choices that didn't align with what he thought I should do—like getting baptized at a different church instead of his—people turned on me. Suddenly, I was ungrateful. Suddenly, the help I'd received was used as leverage, as proof that I owed them something more than gratitude.

It was confusing. Painful. I needed the help, but I also felt trapped by it.

Can you imagine that?

A day that was supposed to be one of the most meaningful of my life—my baptism—became something else entirely. Instead of joy, there was tension. Instead of celebration, there was judgment. Instead of feeling supported, I felt opposed.

Years later, Mr. Murdoch and I reconciled about what happened. We both apologized for how everything unfolded. In that conversation, I found not just understanding, but a small step toward healing.

Still, the experience stayed with me. It taught me something I hadn't understood before- that help isn't always simple. Some people give because they care. Others give because it gives them a sense of power, or because it places you in their debt.

And sometimes, the people who help you can hurt you just as badly as the people who abuse you—just in different ways.

THE COST OF SURVIVAL

Living through constant physical abuse changes you.

It makes you hyper-vigilant. You're always watching, always waiting for the next blow. You learn to read body language, to sense shifts in mood, to make yourself small and quiet in hopes of avoiding attention.

It makes you doubt your worth. When the person who's supposed to love you most treats you like you're disposable, like you're a problem to be managed with violence, you start to believe it. You start to think maybe you deserve it, maybe you really are as terrible as they say.

It makes you afraid of your own anger.

I was terrified of becoming like her. Terrified that, one day, I'd snap and hurt someone the way I'd been hurt. So I swallowed my rage. I pushed it down. I never let myself get angry, even when anger was justified.

And it makes you lonely. Because how do you explain this to anyone? How do you tell your friends that your mother beats you so badly you can't come to school? How do you walk around with bruises and pretend everything is fine?

You can't. So you self-isolate. You keep the truth buried. You survive alone.

The loneliness of abuse is one of its cruelest aspects. It's not just the physical pain—it's the isolation, the shame, the feeling that no one understands and no one cares. It's the weight of carrying a secret that's too heavy for a child to bear.

LEARNING WHAT LOVE IS NOT

Growing up, I learned a distorted version of love. I learned that love hurts. That love is violent. That love is something you survive, rather than something that nourishes you. I learned that love is conditional. That it can be taken away at any moment. That you have to earn it by being good enough, quiet enough, invisible enough. I learned that love comes with fear. That the people who love you can also be the people you're most afraid of.

These lessons stayed with me for years. They shaped the way I saw relationships, the way I let people treat me, and the way I treated myself.

It took a long time—and I'm still learning—to unlearn those lies. To understand that real love doesn't look like what I experienced as a child.

Real love is gentle. It's patient. It's kind. It doesn't keep a record of wrongs. It doesn't delight in tearing you down. It builds you up. It protects. It believes the best about you.

Psalm 34:18 says, *"The Lord is close to the brokenhearted and saves those who are crushed in spirit."*

That scripture became my anchor. It reminded me that, even though human love had failed me—even though the love I should have received from my mother and father was twisted into violence—God's love was different. His love was real. His love didn't come with conditions or violence or betrayal.

He was close to me when I was brokenhearted. He was saving me even when I felt crushed beyond repair.

THE SCARS THAT REMAIN

Physical scars fade, but the emotional and spiritual scars from abuse last much longer.

Even now, I struggle with feeling like I deserve good things. I struggle to accept help without waiting for the other shoe to drop, without wondering what I'll owe in return.

I struggle with trust. It's hard to let people close when the people who were supposed to be closest to you hurt you the most.

I struggle with boundaries. Because I never had any growing up—my body wasn't my own, my space wasn't my own, my safety wasn't guaranteed—I have trouble setting them now. I let people take advantage of me. I say yes when I should say no. I put others' needs before my own, even when it costs me my peace.

These are the wounds that don't show up on X-rays or in photographs. But they're real. And they're still healing.

Healing from abuse isn't linear. Some days, you feel strong, like you've moved past it. Other days, something small—a raised voice, a sudden movement, a familiar smell—takes you right back to that place of fear and pain.

But healing is still possible. It's slow. It's messy. It requires patience, grace, and often professional help. But it's possible.

FORGIVENESS WITHOUT FORGETTING

People often ask me if I've forgiven my mother.

The answer is yes. I have.

But forgiveness doesn't mean forgetting. It doesn't mean pretending it didn't happen, or that it didn't hurt. It doesn't mean excusing her actions, or saying they were okay.

Forgiveness means releasing the hold that anger and bitterness have on my life. It means choosing not to carry the weight of hatred in my heart. It means trusting God to deal with the injustice rather than trying to seek revenge myself.

I've forgiven her, because holding onto unforgiveness was destroying me more than it was hurting her. It was keeping me bound to the past, unable to move forward.

But I also acknowledge that what she did was wrong. That it hurt me deeply. That it left scars I'm still healing from.

Both things can be true.

Forgiveness is not weakness. It's not saying, "What you did was okay." It's saying, "What you did hurt me, but I'm not going to let it control the rest of my life." It's reclaiming your power. It's choosing freedom over bondage.

WHEN GOD VINDICATES

There's a promise in Scripture that God will vindicate His people. That He sees every injustice, every tear, every wound. That nothing goes unnoticed or unpunished.

Romans 12:19 says, *"Do not take revenge, my dear friends, but leave room for God's wrath, for it is written: 'It is mine to avenge; I will repay,' says the Lord."*

I hold onto that promise.

Not because I want my mother or people who did me wrong to suffer. Not because I'm waiting for some cosmic payback. But because I trust that God is just. He sees what happened to me. He cares about the abuse I endured. And in His time, in His way, He will make things right.

That doesn't mean my mother will necessarily face earthly consequences. But it does mean that God knows. He saw every beating. He counted every bruise. He heard every cry.

And He's holding me together even now, helping me heal from wounds that should have destroyed me.

Trusting God to avenge doesn't mean being passive about injustice. It means recognizing that ultimate justice belongs to Him. It means I don't have to carry the burden of making things right—I can focus on healing while He handles the rest.

THE BRIDGE FORWARD

The physical abuse at home was devastating. But the violence I faced wasn't limited to the walls of my house. Outside, the world was just as brutal—maybe even more so.

Because while my mother's fists left bruises that eventually faded, the words and actions of my peers left marks that went even deeper. They attacked not just my body, but my identity. They sought to strip me of dignity, of belonging, of any sense that I had a right to exist.

The bullying I faced at school and in my community became another layer of survival I had to navigate. And it nearly broke me.

SCRIPTURE ANCHOR

"The Lord is close to the brokenhearted and saves those who are crushed in spirit."

— Psalm 34:18 (NIV)

"Do not take revenge, my dear friends, but leave room for God's wrath, for it is written: 'It is mine to avenge; I will repay,' says the Lord."

— Romans 12:19 (NIV)

KEY LESSON

Even when betrayal and abuse try to redefine your worth, God's presence restores the truth: you are loved, valuable, and never forsaken. Abuse distorts our understanding of love, but healing teaches us what real love looks like—gentle, patient, and without conditions. Forgiveness is not forgetting or excusing; it is releasing the hold that bitterness has on your life and trusting God with justice.

REFLECTION MOMENT

Pause and consider: Have you experienced betrayal from people who should have protected you? How has that shaped your understanding of love and trust? What would it look like to release the weight of unforgiveness and trust God with the justice you deserve?

Write down one person or situation you need to forgive—not for their sake, but for your own freedom.

CHAPTER 5

BULLIED, BRANDED, AND BRAVELY WALKING

BEING DIFFERENT IN A WORLD THAT DEMANDS CONFORMITY comes with its own set of battles.

From a young age, I learned that standing out made me a target. My personality, my mannerisms, the way I carried myself—all of it drew attention. And not the good kind.

In Jamaica, masculinity is rigidly defined. Boys are expected to be tough, aggressive, interested in sports, loud, and dominant. Any deviation from that template is seen as a weakness. As wrongness. As something to be mocked, corrected, or eliminated.

I didn't fit the template.

And for that, I paid dearly.

THE SCHOOLYARD BATTLEFIELD

School should have been a safe place. A place to learn, to grow, to discover who I was becoming. Instead, it became a battlefield where I fought daily just to survive.

From primary school through high school, I was relentlessly bullied. The boys at school were ruthless. They mocked the way I walked, the way I talked, the way I expressed myself. They made it clear, day after day, that I didn't belong.

I dreaded going to school. Every morning felt like preparing for war. I'd wake up with my stomach in knots, anxiety twisting through me like a living thing. I'd walk to school slowly, dragging my feet, praying for some miracle that would make the day easier.

The miracle never came.

What people don't understand about bullying is that it's not just the individual incidents—it's the cumulative weight. One insult might not break you. But hundreds of them, day after day, year after year? They crush you. They make you question everything about yourself. They make you wonder if maybe they're right. Maybe you are wrong. Maybe you don't deserve to exist.

PUBLIC HUMILIATION AS ENTERTAINMENT

The worst part wasn't even the physical harassment—it was the public nature of it all.

Nothing about my humiliation was private. The boys who bullied me made sure of that. They called out slurs loud enough for the entire class to hear. Started chants in the cafeteria. Made jokes about me that spread through the school like wildfire.

And people laughed.

Not just the bullies, other students too. Even some who had been friendly to me one-on-one would join once it became public. Because, at that moment, laughing was safer than defending me. Mocking me meant they weren't the target.

I had a few friends defend me at school, and my cousins always encouraged me to stay strong and to continue to be myself, but the consensus was the same. I became a source of entertainment. A punchline. The kid everyone knew it was okay to make fun of because everyone else was doing it.

The shame was suffocating. I couldn't walk down the street without feeling eyes on me, hearing whispers, knowing that somewhere, someone was talking about me, laughing at me, spreading rumors about who I was or what I'd supposedly done.

I wanted to disappear. I wanted to be invisible. I wanted to wake up one day and be someone—anyone—else.

One evening in high school, I was on the bus, in the front, heading home, while a group of boys in the back took turns hurling insults. I just took it, even though I was screaming inside. Because fighting back would have made it worse. Because I'd learned that survival sometimes means making yourself small and enduring.

Shame is a powerful weapon. It doesn't just hurt in the moment—it gets inside you. It becomes part of your internal dialogue. It shapes how you see yourself. And when enough people tell you things about yourself, you start to believe it, even if they're not true.

WHEN SURVIVAL BECOMES YOUR IDENTITY

After years of bullying, something shifted in me.

I stopped trying to defend myself. I stopped hoping that things would change. I stopped believing that people would see me for who I really was and decide I was worth protecting.

Instead, I learned to survive.

I learned to keep my head down. To avoid eye contact. To make myself invisible whenever possible. I learned which streets to walk down and which to avoid. I learned which groups of boys were the most dangerous, and which ones might leave me alone if I stayed out of their way.

I learned to laugh when they made jokes about me, to play along, to act like their words didn't hurt. Because showing pain only encouraged them. Showing vulnerability was like pouring blood in shark-infested water.

I learned to cry in private. To save my tears for the bathroom floor at night, where no one could see, where no one could use my weakness against me.

Survival became my identity. I wasn't Dwayne the student, Dwayne the son, Dwayne the friend. I was Dwayne the survivor. The one who endured. The one who took hit after hit and somehow kept standing.

But survival isn't the same as living. And I wasn't living. I was just existing, day after day, waiting for something—anything—to change.

When you're in survival mode for long enough, you forget what it's like to thrive. You forget what it's like to feel safe, to feel joy, to feel like you have a future worth looking forward to. Your world shrinks to the next moment, the next day, the next week. You lose the ability to dream because dreaming feels dangerous when you're just trying to survive.

THE MOMENTS I ALMOST GAVE UP

There were times when I didn't want to keep going.

Times when the weight of the bullying, combined with everything else I was dealing with at home, felt too heavy to carry. Times when I thought seriously about ending it all, about finding a way out of the pain that seemed to have no end.

I'd stand at the edge of a gully and stare down into the darkness, wondering what would happen if I just let go. I'd hold pills in my hand and count them, calculating whether it would be enough. I'd think about ways to disappear, to make the pain stop, to finally rest.

But something always stopped me.

Sometimes, it was fear. Fear of what comes after death. Fear of hell. Fear of the unknown.

Sometimes, it was a small spark of hope—faint, barely there, but present. A voice that whispered, *This won't last forever. Hold on just a little longer.*

Sometimes, it was my grandmother's and great-grandmother's prayers. I'd hear them praying for me in the early morning hours, calling my name before God, pleading for His protection over my life. And I'd think, *I can't do this to her. I can't break her heart like that.*

And sometimes, I believe it was God Himself, reaching down in those darkest moments and holding me, even when I couldn't feel Him.

Suicidal thoughts are one of the cruelest forms of suffering because they make you believe that the only way out of pain is death. They rob you of hope, of perspective, of the ability to see that things can change. But I'm proof that they can.

I'm proof that you can stand on the edge and choose to step back. That you can hold the pills and choose to put them down. That you can survive the darkest night and wake up to see the sun again.

THE SCRIPTURE THAT HELD ME

Isaiah 54:17 became my anchor during those years: *"'No weapon formed against you shall prosper, and every tongue which rises against you in judgment you shall condemn. This is the heritage of the servants of the Lord, and their righteousness is from Me,' says the Lord."*

I didn't fully understand that scripture when I first heard it. But I held onto it anyway.

No weapon formed against me shall prosper.

The bullies were a weapon. The insults were a weapon. The rejection, the isolation, the constant assault on my identity—all weapons.

But they wouldn't prosper. They wouldn't have the final say.

Every tongue that rises against me in judgment, I shall condemn.

Every person who spoke lies about me, who judged me, who tried to define who I was based on their limited understanding—I had the authority to condemn those words. To reject them. To say, "No, that's not who I am."

That scripture reminded me that my identity wasn't determined by the bullies or the community or even my own self-doubt. It was determined by God.

And in His eyes, I was loved. Chosen. Protected. Destined for something greater than the pain I was walking through.

Scripture has a way of anchoring you when everything else is shifting. It's not magic—it doesn't make the pain disappear. But it gives you something to hold onto when the storm is raging. It reminds you of truths that are bigger than your circumstances.

THE IRONY OF TIME

Years have passed since those days of being bullied.

Many of the boys who tormented me? Some of them aren't even alive anymore. They died young—victims of violence, of the same toxic masculinity they used to measure everyone else. They lived by the sword, and they died by it.

Others have reached out to me over the years. They've tried to be friendly, to act as if nothing happened, to reconnect as if the past doesn't matter. Some have even asked for help—financial help, connections, prayers, opportunities.

The irony isn't lost on me.

It's strange, being in a position where the people who once made my life hell now see me as someone worth knowing. Someone who made it out. Someone who succeeded, despite everything they did to break me.

I don't gloat. I don't throw their past behavior in their faces. But I also don't forget. I forgive, but I remember. And I'm careful about who I let into my life now.

Because I've learned that not everyone who wants access to you deserves it.

Time has a way of revealing truth. The same people who mocked you for being different will later come to you for help, because that difference became your strength. The same people who said you'd never amount to anything will watch you succeed and wonder how you did it. Don't let their change of heart make you doubt the validity of your pain. What they did was real. What you survived was real. And you don't owe them anything.

CHOOSING COURAGE OVER CONFORMITY

The bullying tried to break me. It tried to force me to conform, to become someone I wasn't, to erase the parts of me that made me different.

But it failed.

Not because I was naturally strong. Not because I had some super-human ability to withstand abuse. But because somewhere deep inside, even in my darkest moments, there was a part of me that refused to give up.

A part of me that said, *You are more than what they say you are.*

A part of me that believed, against all evidence, that there was a future worth fighting for.

That part kept me alive. It kept me moving forward. It kept me showing up, day after day, even when everything in me wanted to quit.

And over time, that small act of showing up—of refusing to let them win—became my strength.

I learned that courage isn't the absence of fear. It's moving forward *despite* the fear. It's showing up to school even though you know you'll be mocked. It's walking down the street with your head up, even though you know people are watching. It's being yourself even when the world tells you that yourself isn't acceptable.

That's bravery. And I learned it the hard way.

Courage is often quiet. It doesn't always look like standing up and fighting back. Sometimes, it looks like surviving another day. Sometimes, it looks like getting out of bed when you don't want to. Sometimes, it looks like choosing to live when death feels easier. Don't underestimate the courage it takes just to keep going.

THE BRIDGE FORWARD

The bullying taught me hard lessons about human nature. About how people treat those who are different. About how cruelty can become normalized, even celebrated, in communities that fear what they don't understand.

But it also taught me something I didn't expect: Not everyone who claims to care about you actually does.

Betrayal wasn't just something I experienced from strangers and bullies. It came from people I trusted. People I called friends. People who knew my story and used it against me.

The next layer of my survival wasn't just about enduring attacks from enemies—it was about recognizing wolves in sheep's clothing. It was about learning that, sometimes, the people closest to you can hurt you the most.

SCRIPTURE ANCHOR

"'No weapon formed against you shall prosper, and every tongue which rises against you in judgment you shall condemn. This is the heritage of the servants of the Lord, and their righteousness is from Me,' says the Lord."
— Isaiah 54:17 (NKJV)

KEY LESSON

The words of others can wound, but they do not have the power to define your identity or destiny. God has the final say, and His promises are stronger than the judgments of people. Courage is not the absence of fear—it's the decision to move forward even when fear is present. What feels like weakness in the moment (surviving, enduring, simply showing up) is actually profound strength. Your difference is not a flaw to be fixed, but a gift to be embraced.

REFLECTION MOMENT

Take time to reflect: When have you been ridiculed, mocked, or bullied? How have those experiences shaped your sense of self, and how can you begin to reclaim your courage and identity from the voices that sought to diminish you?

Write down one lie you believed about yourself because of bullying, and beside it, write the truth about who God says you are.

____

____

____

____

____

____

____

____

____

____

____

____

____

____

CHAPTER 6

FRIENDS, OR WOLVES?

ONE OF THE HARDEST LESSONS I LEARNED GROWING UP WAS that not everyone who smiles at you is a friend. Some people come into your life with good intentions. Some are fleeting, meant for a season. And some are wolves in sheep's clothing—hiding their true nature until the moment is right to strike.

I gave my genuine self to people. I trusted. I loved. I believed in friendship. And yet, I was betrayed. Over and over again.

Lies were spread about me. Gossip became a weapon used to tarnish my character. People I thought would have my back showed their true colors in ways that cut deeper than any insult from a stranger.

THE LONELINESS OF NEEDING FRIENDSHIP

When you grow up in an environment where you're constantly rejected, you become desperate for connection. For someone—anyone—to see you and accept you.

I wanted friends so badly. I wanted to belong. I wanted to be part of something, to have people I could trust, to know what it felt like to be chosen.

So when people showed me even the smallest amount of kindness, I held onto it. I ignored red flags. I made excuses for behavior that should have warned me away. I gave people access to my heart, my story, my vulnerabilities—because I thought that's what friendship required.

But I was wrong.

Not everyone who asks about your life genuinely cares. Not everyone who offers help has pure motives. And not everyone who calls you "friend" actually wants what's best for you.

Desperation makes you vulnerable. When you're starving for love and acceptance, you'll take crumbs from anyone who offers them. You'll overlook mistreatment because at least it's attention. You'll tolerate betrayal because at least you're not alone.

But that's not friendship. That's survival disguised as connection.

FAKE PAGES AND FALSE FRIENDS

One of the most painful betrayals came through social media.

Someone created a fake profile—pretending to be someone interested in getting to know me. They messaged me, asked questions, and seemed genuinely curious about my life. And I, desperate for connection, opened up.

I shared things I wouldn't normally share. Personal details. Struggles I was facing. Thoughts and feelings I'd kept hidden from most people.

And then the truth came out.

It wasn't a genuine person on the other side of that profile. It was someone I knew—someone trying to gather information, to find ammunition, to collect details they could use against me later.

When I found out, the shame was overwhelming. I felt violated. Exposed. Foolish for having trusted someone who was clearly using me.

I couldn't believe it. Why would someone go to such lengths just to hurt me? What had I done to deserve that level of cruelty?

But that's the thing about wolves—they don't need a reason. Sometimes, people hurt others simply because they can. Because it makes them feel powerful. Because they're operating from their own brokenness, and they want to spread that pain to someone else.

Betrayal from a stranger hurts. But betrayal from someone you trusted—someone you let into your inner world—that's a different kind of pain. It makes you question your judgment. It makes you afraid to trust again. It makes you want to build walls so high that no one can ever hurt you like that again.

THE GOSSIP NETWORK

My community thrived on gossip. It was currency. Entertainment. A way for people to feel superior by tearing others down.

And I was a favorite topic.

People talked about me constantly. They speculated about my identity, my relationships. They made up stories when the truth wasn't interesting enough. They exaggerated, twisted facts, and created entire narratives about who I was—none of which were accurate, but all of which spread like wildfire.

Right now, this spirit runs rampant, taking hold of people. Many do not understand that it can lead to their destruction. It's important to be mindful of what you say about people, because your children may have to deal with the consequences. As my grandmother would say, "If you have nothing good to say, keep yuh mouth shut."

Gossip is violence. It destroys reputations, relationships, and, sometimes, lives. And the people who engage in it often don't see themselves as doing anything wrong. They justify it as "concern," or "just telling the truth," or "sharing prayer requests." But the Bible is clear: Gossip is sin. And it destroys.

CONFRONTATION: THE STRUGGLE I CARRIED

Looking back, one of my biggest struggles was confrontation—or rather, my inability to do it.

I hated confrontation. I avoided it at all costs. Even when people hurt me, even when I knew they'd betrayed me, I couldn't bring myself to address it directly. I'd rather just cut people off silently than have an uncomfortable conversation. I'd rather disappear from their life than explain why I was hurt, or say nothing at all, even though I knew everything.

Part of it was fear. Fear of conflict. Fear of making things worse. Fear that if I spoke up, I'd be the one who ended up looking bad.

Part of it was low self-worth. I didn't believe I had the right to demand better treatment. I didn't think my feelings mattered enough to defend.

And part of it was exhaustion. After years of fighting just to survive, I didn't have energy left for confronting every person who hurt me.

But avoiding confrontation came with a cost.

It meant I carried resentment. It meant I built walls that kept everyone out, not just the people who deserved to be kept out. It meant I never gave people the chance to make things right, to explain, to grow.

And it meant I never learned to advocate for myself, to set boundaries, to communicate what I needed in relationships.

I'm still learning this lesson. Still learning that confrontation, done in love and with respect, isn't something to fear—it's something necessary. It's how we protect ourselves. It's how we set boundaries. It's how we give people the opportunity to do better.

And if I can't communicate with the people I can see, how can I expect to communicate effectively with God, whom I can't see? Communication is foundational to all relationships—including our relationship with Him.

LEARNING DISCERNMENT THE HARD WAY

I didn't have discernment when I was younger. I didn't know how to read people or see certain things. I took everyone at face value, assumed the best, and trusted too easily.

That naivety cost me.

But over time—through betrayal after betrayal, lesson after painful lesson—I learned.

I learned to pay attention to patterns, not just words. People can say anything. But their actions tell the truth.

I learned to watch how people treat others, not just how they treat me. If someone gossips to you about others, they're gossiping to others about you.

I learned that when someone shows you who they are, believe them. Don't make excuses for them. Don't rationalize their behavior. Don't give them endless chances to hurt you in the same way.

I learned that not everyone deserves access to my life. That it's okay to keep some things private. That I don't owe people my story, my time, or my energy just because they ask for it.

Proverbs 27:6 says, *"Wounds from a friend can be trusted, but an enemy multiplies kisses."*

That scripture helped me understand the difference between real friends and fake ones. Real friends might hurt you, but their wounds are honest. They come from a place of love, a desire to see you grow, and a willingness to tell you hard truths because they care about your well-being. Fake friends flatter you. They tell you what you want to hear. They multiply kisses—empty gestures that look like care, but are really manipulation.

Learning to tell the difference saved me.

Discernment is a gift from God. It's the ability to see beyond surface appearances, to sense motives and intentions, to recognize truth from lies.

And it's something you develop over time, through experience, through prayer, and through paying attention to the Holy Spirit's gentle warnings.

THE COST OF PEOPLE-PLEASING

One pattern I noticed in my life was people-pleasing. I'd say yes when I wanted to say no. I'd accommodate people even when it cost me my peace. I'd let people into my space when I needed to be alone.

Why? Because I was afraid of disappointing them. Afraid they'd stop liking me. Afraid they'd abandon me like everyone else had.

So I made myself smaller. I sacrificed my needs for theirs. I bent over backwards to make sure everyone else was comfortable, even when I was drowning.

And people took advantage of that.

They'd show up unannounced and expect me to drop everything. They'd ask for favors and never reciprocate. They'd take and take and take, and I'd give and give and give, until I had nothing left.

I remember one incident clearly. A friend texted me late one night saying he was coming to visit—not asking, just informing me.

I wasn't in a good mental space. I needed time alone. But I said nothing.

I spent the night cleaning, preparing, and stressing. I couldn't sleep because I was anxious about having someone in my space when I wasn't ready for it.

When he arrived, I tried to be a good host. But inside, I was resentful. Angry. Frustrated that he hadn't considered my needs, that he'd assumed I'd be available, that he'd put me in this position.

Finally, after days of internal turmoil, I managed to say something. Not confrontationally, but gently: "Hey, I wasn't really in a good space for company. Next time, could you let me know in advance?"

His response was dismissive. Everyone has things going on. Everyone's busy. He minimized my feelings and made it seem like I was overreacting.

And in that moment, I realized: People will treat you however you allow them to treat you.

If you don't set boundaries, they'll keep crossing them. If you don't speak up, they'll keep assuming your silence means consent. If you don't value your own needs, no one else will, either.

People-pleasing isn't kindness. It's self-abandonment. It's prioritizing everyone else's comfort over your own well-being. And it's not sustainable. Eventually, you'll burn out. Eventually, the resentment will consume you. Eventually, you'll have to choose: them or you.

I'm learning to choose me. And that's not selfish—it's necessary.

SETTING BOUNDARIES I SHOULD HAVE SET YEARS AGO

Boundaries have been one of the hardest things for me to establish. Because I grew up without any—my body wasn't my own, my space wasn't my own, my feelings didn't matter—I never learned how to set them.

But I'm learning now.

I'm learning that it's okay to say no. That "No" is a complete sentence. That I don't owe people explanations for my boundaries.

I'm learning that it's okay to need time alone. That solitude isn't the same as loneliness. That I can love people and still need space from them.

I'm learning that it's okay to cut people off who repeatedly disrespect me. That forgiveness doesn't require continued relationship. That I can wish someone well from a distance without letting them back into my life.

I'm learning that healthy relationships have mutual respect. That the people who truly care about me will honor my boundaries, not fight against them.

And I'm learning that I have to love myself enough to protect myself—even when it means disappointing others.

Setting boundaries feels selfish at first, especially when you've spent your whole life accommodating everyone else. But boundaries aren't selfish— they're self-respect. They're saying, "I matter too." They're recognizing that you can't pour from an empty cup, that you can't love others well if you're not loving yourself.

THE FEW WHO STAYED

There were a few—very few—who proved themselves to be real.

My grandmother, who prayed for me even when she couldn't protect me.

My great-grandmother, who offered me refuge when she could, who spoke life over me when the world spoke death.

A teacher here or there who saw something in me and urged me to keep going.

Mr. Murdoch, who helped me financially, my God Mother who supported me, Cousins who stood by me. Strangers who showed unexpected kindness. Friends who poured into me as much as I poured into them.

They weren't many—but they were enough.

They kept me going. Reminded me I wasn't completely alone. Gave me just enough hope to hold on one more day.

I'm grateful for them—even the ones whose help came with complications. Even the ones who weren't perfect. Because I've come to understand that people don't have to be perfect to play a meaningful role in your life.

And I've learned that a small circle of genuine people is worth more than a crowd that disappears when it matters. That it's okay to trust a few deeply, instead of trying to belong everywhere.

Some people are meant to stay. Others come for a season—sometimes to help, sometimes to teach, sometimes to do both. Learning the difference has taken time. Letting go has taken even more but it's necessary for growth.

THE BRIDGE FORWARD

Betrayal taught me to be careful about whom I trust. But it also threatened to close my heart completely. To make me so afraid of being hurt again that I'd never let anyone in.

I had to find a balance between wisdom and openness. Between protecting myself and remaining vulnerable enough to build real connections. But there was another lesson I needed to learn—one that went even deeper than friendship betrayals.

Because while people had failed me in countless ways, there was a basic human need I still hadn't figured out how to meet: There were days I went to school without food, without money, carrying needs I didn't have the words for.

Because hunger—real hunger—has a way of teaching you things no one ever prepares you for.

SCRIPTURE ANCHOR

"Wounds from a friend can be trusted, but an enemy multiplies kisses."
— Proverbs 27:6 (NIV)

KEY LESSON

Discernment is a gift from God that protects you from those who would harm you. True friends are rare, and not everyone who offers help or kindness has pure motives. Learning to set boundaries, communicate your needs, and recognize patterns of behavior are essential skills for emotional and spiritual health. A small circle of genuine relationships is far more valuable than a large network of shallow connections. People-pleasing is not love—it's self-abandonment.

REFLECTION MOMENT

Pause and reflect: Who in your life has proven to be a true friend, and who has shown themself to be a wolf in disguise? Are there relationships you're holding onto out of fear or obligation, rather than genuine connection? What boundaries do you need to set to protect your peace and well-being?

Write down one relationship that needs evaluation and one boundary you need to establish.

CHAPTER 7

WHEN HUNGER TEACHES

School should have been a place of learning, growth, and opportunity. But for me, it was also a place of hunger—both physical and emotional.

I went to school without money, without food, and, often, without hope. Some days, I depended on PATH lunches, the government program in Jamaica that provided meals to children. But even that was inconsistent. Many times, I went without.

Hunger became my constant companion. Not just the gnawing in my stomach, but the deeper hunger for stability, for safety, for a life that didn't require me to beg just to survive.

THE DAILY CALCULATION

Every morning started with the same calculation: Do I have money for lunch today? Do I have bus fare? If I go to school, will I be able to eat?

Most days, the answer was no.

I learned quickly that hunger could either break me or drive me. I chose the latter. I begged when I had to, borrowed when I had no choice, and sometimes, I quietly went without.

I'd ask friends if they had extra food. Some would share. Others would look away, embarrassed or uncomfortable. I learned to read people's faces, to know who I could ask and who would make me feel even more ashamed than I already did.

I'd go to the guidance counselor's office sometimes, hoping for a free lunch ticket. They'd give it to me occasionally, but it wasn't something I could count on every day. And the humiliation of asking—of admitting I didn't have what every other kid seemed to have—was almost worse than the hunger itself.

There were days I sat in class with my stomach cramping, my head light, trying to focus on lessons when all I could think about was food. Days when I watched other kids pull out snacks or lunches their parents had packed, and I felt the weight of my difference, my lack, my shame.

Hunger does something to you. It's not just physical discomfort—it's a reminder of your place in the world. When everyone around you has what they need, and you don't, you feel less than. You feel forgotten. You feel like maybe you don't matter as much as everyone else.

THE DETERMINATION BUILDS

Despite the struggle, I never stopped showing up. I never stopped trying. And even though I cried and prayed through the storm, I clung to the one thing that never failed—my faith in God.

These seasons of hunger shaped more than my stomach; they shaped my character. I developed resilience, determination, and a hunger for more than just food. I was hungry for education, for growth, and for a life that reflected the purpose God had placed inside of me. I refused to let my circumstances define my destiny.

Even as I moved into high school, undergraduate and graduate school, the struggle followed me. Financial limitations, emotional burdens, and isolation were constant companions. But I worked. I saved. I risked. I persevered. And I saw God show up repeatedly, placing people in my life at just the right time to assist me in ways I couldn't have imagined.

When I got to high school and it was time to take my CSEC examinations—the standardized tests required to get into college in Jamaica—I had no money to pay for them. These exams cost money, and without passing them, there was no path forward. No college. No future.

That's when Mr. Murdoch came into my life. He paid for my exam fees. He bought me clothes. He provided financial support when I had nothing. Without him, I might not have been able to finish high school or pursue college.

God sent him in that season. When I needed it most, God provided.

HUNGER THAT FOLLOWS YOU

You'd think that, once I left Jamaica and came to America for graduate school, the hunger would stop. But it didn't.

I came to Miami to attend Nova Southeastern University with just enough money saved to pay for my first semester. That was it. I had no plan for how I'd pay for the remaining semesters, no safety net, no backup.

But I knew one thing: If God starts something in me, He's going to finish it.

So I stepped out in faith. I enrolled. I showed up. And I trusted.

God came through. He granted me a graduate assistantship—a job on campus that paid for most of my tuition and gave me a small stipend. I was able to complete my degree. I still owe Nova Southeastern about $5,000, and they sent my bill to collections. But I graduated. I finished.

And even now, as I write this, I'm in another season of hunger.

I lost my job in August 2025. Got fired. Or maybe more accurately, God redirected me. Because I know—*I know*—that losing that job wasn't random. It was intentional. God was closing a door because He had something else for me.

Right now, as I sit here writing this chapter, I haven't had a job since August 5th. It's been months. My rent is unpaid. I have thousands of dollars in debt. I don't have money for groceries, for bills, for anything.

And yet, I'm still in my apartment. I'm still here.

Every day, I wake up and wonder if today will be the day I get evicted. If today will be the day the lights get shut off. If today will be the day everything falls apart.

But it hasn't. And I believe it won't.

Because even in this wilderness, even in this season of scarcity, I feel God's presence. I hear Him saying, *"Trust Me. I've got you. Haven't I kept you this far?"*

I've been applying for jobs. Doing interviews. Sending out resumes. And I keep getting ghosted. No callbacks. No offers. Just silence.

At first, it frustrated me. Then it discouraged me. Now? Now I'm starting to understand.

God is keeping those doors closed because He's preparing me for something else. He's redirecting me toward ministry, toward preaching, toward the book you're reading right now, toward my prayer CD, toward the calling He placed on my life, and more.

This season isn't about punishment. It's about preparation.

But I won't lie to you—it's hard.

There are days when my faith is strong, when I wake up praising God, confident that He's going to come through. And there are other days when my faith feels nonexistent. When I'm tired. When I'm scared. When I wonder if I heard Him wrong.

That's the reality of walking by faith. It's not always strong. It's not always confident. Sometimes, it's just holding on by a thread and saying, "God, I'm still here. I'm still trusting. Please don't let me fall."

THE SILENCE OF GOD

One of the hardest parts of this season has been God's silence.

I pray. Every day, I pray. I cry out to Him. I ask for direction, for provision, for a sign that I'm on the right path.

And often, I hear nothing.

The silence is deafening. It makes me question everything. Did I hear Him correctly? Is He still with me? Did I do something wrong? Has He abandoned me?

But I'm learning something crucial: **God's silence doesn't mean His absence.**

Sometimes, He's silent because He's already spoken, and He's waiting for me to obey what He's already said. Sometimes, He's silent because He's working behind the scenes, orchestrating things I can't see yet. Sometimes, He's silent because He's teaching me to trust Him without needing constant reassurance.

The Israelites wandered in the wilderness for 40 years. *40 years.* That's a long time. And I'm sure there were moments when they wondered if God had forgotten them, if He'd abandoned them, if they'd ever make it to the promised land.

But they did. Eventually, they crossed over. The season ended. And they entered a land flowing with milk and honey.

My wilderness season will end, too. I believe that. I have to believe that. Because if I don't, I'll give up. And I've come too far to give up now.

Psalm 27:14 says, *"Wait for the Lord; be strong and take heart and wait for the Lord."*

Waiting is active, not passive. It's continuing to do the work, continuing to show up, continuing to trust, even when you can't see the outcome.

HUNGER AS A TEACHER

Looking back over my life, I can see how hunger—both physical and spiritual—has been one of my greatest teachers.

It taught me resilience. It taught me that I'm stronger than I think. That I can endure more than I ever imagined. That survival is built into my DNA.

It taught me compassion. Because I know what it's like to go without, I see people who are struggling in ways others might miss. I notice the kid in the back of the room who never brings lunch. I see the person at church who's trying to hide their need. I recognize the silent hunger that so many people carry.

It taught me gratitude. When you've gone without, you don't take things for granted. Every meal is a blessing. Every paycheck is a miracle. Every provision—no matter how small—is evidence of God's faithfulness.

And it taught me dependence. Not on people, not on systems, not on my own ability—but on God. Because when you have nothing else, when every human option has dried up, God becomes your only source. And you learn that He's more than enough.

Philippians 4:12–13 says, *"I know what it is to be in need, and I know what it is to have plenty. I have learned the secret of being content in any and every situation, whether well fed or hungry, whether living in plenty or in want. I can do all this through him who gives me strength."*

I'm not there yet. I haven't fully learned the secret of contentment. Some days, I'm angry about my circumstances. Some days, I'm frustrated that things aren't moving faster. Some days, I'm tired of fighting.

But I'm learning.

Slowly, painfully, I'm learning that my circumstances don't define God's faithfulness. That provision doesn't always look like money in the bank—sometimes, it looks like peace in the storm. Sometimes, it looks like joy in the struggle. Sometimes, it looks like still being here when by all logic, you shouldn't be.

THE BILLS THAT DON'T STOP

Let me be honest about where I am right now.

My rent hasn't been paid in eight months. That's about $18,000 I owe.

My car payment fell behind—and then the car was gone. Repossessed.

Credit card debt I can't even begin to touch. Student loans. Medical bills. The list doesn't end.

And I have no income.

None.

Every logical part of me says I should be panicking. I should be terrified. I should be doing whatever it takes—taking any job, any opportunity, anything—to make money.

But something in me—something I can only describe as the Holy Spirit—keeps saying, *"Be still. Trust Me. Focus on what I've called you to do right now."*

So that's what I'm doing. Even though it makes no sense financially. Even though it looks foolish from the outside. Even though I don't know how the bills will get paid.

I'm trusting. I'm obeying. God doesn't call you to something without equipping you to walk it out.

Am I scared? Yes. Do I have moments where I wonder if I'm crazy? Absolutely. But do I believe God is going to come through? Yes. Because He always has. And I don't believe He's brought me this far just to let me fall now.

WHAT HUNGER REVEALS

Hunger—whether physical, financial, or spiritual—has a way of revealing what's really inside you.

It reveals your priorities. When you can't have everything, you figure out what matters most. And in this season, what matters most to me is my obedience to God. Not comfort. Not security. Not financial stability. Obedience.

It reveals your faith. It's easy to say you trust God when everything is going well. But when you're in lack, when there's no backup plan, when it's literally just you and God? That's when you find out if your faith is real.

It reveals your character. Do you become bitter and resentful? Do you blame God? Do you give up? Or do you keep going, keep trusting, keep believing that there's purpose in the pain?

And it reveals God's faithfulness. Because even in the leanest seasons, even when I couldn't see a way forward, God provided. Maybe not how I expected. Maybe not when I wanted. But He provided.

He's still providing. Even now, as I write this with an empty bank account and overdue bills, I'm still here. I still have a roof over my head. I still have food to eat. I still have the strength to keep going.

That's not luck. That's not coincidence. That's God.

A WORD TO THOSE IN THE WILDERNESS

If you're reading this and you're in a season of hunger—financial, emotional, spiritual—I want you to know something:

This season won't last forever.

It feels like it will. When you're in it, when you're living it day after day, it feels endless. It feels like you're stuck, like there's no way out, like things will never change.

But they will. Seasons shift. Doors open. Provision comes. Not always in the way we expect, not always in the timing we want, but it comes.

The Israelites spent 40 years in the wilderness, but they didn't stay there. They crossed over.

And you will too.

Your promised land might not look like financial wealth. It might not look like a perfect job or a comfortable life. But it will look like peace. Like purpose. Like finally understanding why you had to go through what you went through.

So hold on. Keep praying, even when it feels like God isn't listening. Keep showing up, even when you're exhausted. Keep trusting, even when your faith feels weak.

Because the God who sees you, who knows exactly what you need, who has carried you this far—He's not going to abandon you now.

Matthew 6:26 reminds us, *"Look at the birds of the air; they do not sow or reap or store away in barns, and yet your heavenly Father feeds them. Are you not much more valuable than they?"*

If God feeds the birds, He'll feed you. If He clothes the lilies, He'll clothe you. If He's brought you through every other wilderness season, He'll bring you through this one too.

THE BRIDGE FORWARD

Hunger taught me to fight for survival. But there was another kind of hunger I carried for years—a hunger I didn't fully understand until much later.

It was a hunger for love. For acceptance. For someone to see me and decide I was worth choosing.

That hunger led me to search in places I shouldn't have searched. To settle for relationships that hurt me, because at least they filled the void temporarily. To confuse attention with affection, and physical connection with emotional intimacy.

I was hungry for love, but I didn't know what real love looked like. So I kept looking in all the wrong places, hoping that, eventually, I'd find what I was searching for.

SCRIPTURE ANCHOR

"I know what it is to be in need, and I know what it is to have plenty. I have learned the secret of being content in any and every situation, whether well fed or hungry, whether living in plenty or in want. I can do all this through him who gives me strength."

— Philippians 4:12–13 (NIV)

"Look at the birds of the air; they do not sow or reap or store away in barns, and yet your heavenly Father feeds them. Are you not much more valuable than they?"

— Matthew 6:26 (NIV)

KEY LESSON

Seasons of lack are not meant to destroy you, but to prepare you. Hunger—whether physical, financial, or spiritual—can sharpen your vision, strengthen your faith, and fuel your determination to keep pressing toward purpose.

God's silence does not mean His absence; sometimes, He is working most powerfully in the moments when we hear Him least. Provision doesn't always look like abundance—sometimes, it looks like just enough, given at just the right time.

REFLECTION MOMENT

Pause and consider: What are you hungry for in your life right now? Are your struggles shaping determination within you, or are they holding you back? How can you rely on God to provide strength and guidance through your seasons of scarcity?

Write down one area of lack you're facing, and beside it, write one way God has already shown His faithfulness in your life.

THE VOID AND THE VINE

Growing up without love from the people who were supposed to protect and nurture me left a deep void. I craved attention, care, and acceptance, but I didn't know how to receive them in healthy ways. I was drawn to people and places that offered a semblance of love, even when it wasn't genuine.

I chased relationships for validation. I sought approval from friends, peers, and even strangers, because my heart longed to be seen, acknowledged, and valued. I gave my trust easily, and often too soon, because I had learned to fend for myself at a young age. Yet, many of these connections were temporary, shallow, or even harmful.

THE DESPERATE SEARCH FOR BELONGING

When you grow up feeling unwanted, you become desperate for someone—anyone—to want you.

I looked for love everywhere. In friendships that weren't really friendships. In relationships that were built on need rather than genuine connection. In people who showed me even the smallest amount of kindness, because I was so starved for affection that crumbs felt like a feast.

I didn't know what healthy love looked like. All I knew was what I didn't have. And that void inside me—that gaping hole left by a mother who couldn't love me, a father who was absent, a community that rejected me—it screamed for something to fill it.

So I filled it with whatever I could find. Attention from people who didn't actually care about me. Validation from people who were using me. Physical connection that felt like intimacy, but was really just two broken people trying to ease their loneliness for a moment.

I gave pieces of myself to people who didn't deserve them. I let people in who should have been kept out. I stayed in situations that hurt me, because I thought that pain was better than being alone.

Looking back, I see now that I was trying to fill a God-sized void with human-sized solutions. And it never worked. It couldn't work. Because people—no matter how well-meaning—can't fill a space that was designed for God alone.

THE SENSITIVITY I TRIED TO HIDE

I've always been sensitive. Even as a child, I felt things deeply. I cried easily. I took things to heart. I cared—sometimes, too much.

And I hated that about myself.

In a world that values toughness, that tells boys to "man up" and "stop being so soft," sensitivity felt like a weakness. It felt like another way I didn't measure up, another way I was different from everyone else.

I tried to hide it. I tried to toughen up, to not let things affect me, to pretend I didn't care when people hurt me. But I couldn't. I felt everything. Every harsh word. Every rejection. Every betrayal.

And because I was so sensitive, I treated people the way I wanted to be treated. I was careful with my words because I knew how much words could hurt. I was thoughtful in my actions because I understood how much actions could impact someone. I gave grace because I desperately wanted grace given to me.

But the world didn't operate that way. People weren't as careful with me as I was with them. They said things without thinking about the impact. They took what I gave and rarely gave back. They used my sensitivity against me, seeing it as a flaw rather than a strength.

For years, I thought something was wrong with me. I thought I needed to change, to become harder, to stop caring so much.

I'm learning now that my sensitivity isn't a weakness—it's a gift. It's what allows me to see people's pain when others miss it. It's what allows me to offer compassion to those who are hurting. It's what makes me a good friend, a good listener, a safe space for people who need one.

The problem wasn't that I was too sensitive. The problem was that I was surrounded by people who weren't sensitive enough. People who had built walls so high around their hearts that they couldn't recognize genuine care when they saw it.

FINDING PEOPLE WHO MATCH YOUR HEART

In recent years, God has brought a few people into my life who match my energy. Who are sensitive like me. Who care deeply like I do. Who value genuine connection and aren't afraid of emotional depth.

And with those people, I don't have to hide. I don't have to pretend. I don't have to tone myself down or apologize for feeling things deeply.

With the right people, my sensitivity is celebrated, not criticized. It's seen as a strength, not a flaw.

That's taught me something important: **You're not too much for the right people. You're only too much for the wrong ones.**

If someone makes you feel like you're too sensitive, too emotional, too intense—that's not your problem. That's a sign that they're not your person.

The right people will appreciate your heart. They'll value your depth. They'll treasure the fact that you care as much as you do.

Proverbs 27:19 says, "As water reflects the face, so one's life reflects the heart." My sensitivity is a reflection of my heart. And I'm learning to protect that heart by being more discerning about who I let close to it.

POURING OUT WHEN YOUR CUP IS EMPTY

One of the patterns I've noticed in my life is that I'm always pouring out. I pour out emotionally for people who need someone to talk to. I pour out spiritually for people who need prayer or encouragement. I pour out financially when I have it, being a helping hand, giving to people who are in need, even when I'm barely making it myself.

I pour and pour and pour. And often, I end up empty.

And then I wonder: Who pours into me? When I'm the one who's struggling, who shows up? When I'm the one who needs encouragement, who's there to give it?

The answer, more often than not, has been: no one.

Not because people are intentionally neglectful. But because most people are so consumed with their own struggles that they don't have the capacity to pour into someone else. Or because they assume I'm strong enough that I don't need it. Or because they've gotten so used to me being the giver that they don't think about giving back.

And I can't lie—it hurts. It makes me feel used. It makes me feel like people only value me for what I can do for them, not for who I am.

But I'm learning something in this season: **God is my primary source, not people.**

Yes, God uses people to bless me, to encourage me, to pour into me. And I'm grateful for the few who do. But I can't depend on people to fill me up. I have to go to God for that. I have to let Him be my source of strength, of encouragement, of provision.

When I pour out of an overflow that comes from Him, I don't run dry. But when I pour out of my own reserves, expecting people to refill me, I end up depleted and disappointed.

2 Corinthians 9:8 says, "And God is able to bless you abundantly, so that in all things at all times, having all that you need, you will abound in every good work." My ability to pour out isn't dependent on what people give me—it's dependent on what God gives me. And His supply is endless.

SEEKING LOVE IN ALL THE WRONG PLACES

I'm not going to pretend I've been perfect. I've made mistakes. I've sinned. I've struggled with things I'm not comfortable talking about openly—sexual sin, seeking validation through physical connection, trying to fill the void with things that were never meant to fill it.

And the shame of those mistakes was heavy. Because on one hand, I was someone who loved God, who wanted to serve Him, who felt called to ministry. But on the other hand, I was someone who was broken—someone who struggled, who at times fell into the same patterns over and over again.

This used to be one of my biggest battles. There were times when I thought I had it under control—when I was walking in obedience and staying strong—but certain triggers—stress, loneliness, fear—would pull me back into old habits: pornography, masturbation, and seeking connection in ways I knew weren't right.

And then the guilt would come. The shame.

Every time I tried to fight those battles in my own strength, I failed. But when I surrendered to God—when I allowed the Holy Spirit to strengthen me, when I chose obedience even when I didn't feel strong enough—that's when I began to experience real breakthrough.

1 Corinthians 10:13 says, "No temptation has overtaken you except what is common to mankind. And God is faithful; he will not let you be tempted beyond what you can bear. But when you are tempted, he will also provide a way out so that you can endure it."

The way out isn't willpower. It wasn't trying harder or doing better. The way out is the Holy Spirit- leaning into His strength when mine ran out, being honest about my weakness and letting Him be strong in it.

THE LOVE THAT NEVER FAILS

Through all the failed relationships, all the disappointment, all the searching in the wrong places, I've come to understand something crucial:

The only love that will ever truly satisfy me is God's love.

Human love is imperfect. It fails. It disappoints. It changes. It's conditional, even when people claim it's not.

But God's love? It's perfect. It's unchanging. It's unconditional. It's everlasting.

Jeremiah 31:3 says, *"The Lord appeared to us in the past, saying: 'I have loved you with an everlasting love; I have drawn you with unfailing kindness.'"*

Everlasting. Unfailing. That's the kind of love I was searching for all along. And I was looking for it in people who could never provide it, because they weren't designed to.

People are meant to *reflect* God's love, not replace it. They're meant to be *conduits* of His love, not the source of it.

And when I finally started seeking God's love first—when I stopped trying to fill the void with human connection and started letting God fill it—something shifted.

I stopped being so desperate for approval. I stopped settling for relationships that hurt me. I stopped giving pieces of myself to people who didn't value them.

Because I finally understood: **I am loved. Fully. Completely. Unconditionally. By the God who created me, who knows me, who sees every broken part of me and loves me anyway.**

That doesn't mean I don't still struggle. It doesn't mean I've arrived. But it does mean I have an anchor. A foundation. A source of love that never runs dry.

THE BRIDGE FORWARD

Learning to find my worth in God rather than in people was a crucial step. But knowing something intellectually and living it out are two different things.

Because even as I learned to anchor my identity in Christ, there were still battles raging inside me. Battles in my mind. Dark thoughts. Spiritual warfare. Moments when I didn't just want to give up—I wanted to disappear entirely.

The next layer of my journey wasn't just about finding love. It was about finding the will to keep living when everything in me wanted to quit.

SCRIPTURE ANCHOR

"The Lord appeared to us in the past, saying: 'I have loved you with an everlasting love; I have drawn you with unfailing kindness.'"
— JEREMIAH 31:3 (NIV)

"And God is able to bless you abundantly, so that in all things at all times, having all that you need, you will abound in every good work."
— 2 CORINTHIANS 9:8 (NIV)

KEY LESSON

The love we often crave from others can never fill the void that only God's everlasting love can satisfy. Sensitivity is not a flaw, but a gift that allows for deeper compassion and connection with others. When we anchor ourselves in His love, we gain the strength to recognize, receive, and give love in its truest form. People-pleasing is not love—it's self-abandonment. Learning to set boundaries and communicate needs is essential for healthy relationships and spiritual growth.

REFLECTION MOMENT

Take time to reflect: Where in your life have you sought love or validation from the wrong sources? How has your sensitivity—whether seen as strength or weakness—shaped your relationships? What would it look like to anchor your worth in God's love rather than in people's approval?

Write down one boundary you need to set and one way you can begin to receive God's love more fully.

CHAPTER 9

WHEN THE MIND BATTLES

There were moments in my life when the darkness felt too heavy to bear.

Thoughts of ending it all crept into my mind more than once. I felt overwhelmed, trapped in a circle of pain, confusion, and despair. The abuse, rejection, and loneliness I had endured weighed on me like a relentless storm, threatening to swallow me whole.

But even in the darkest nights, prayer became my lifeline. Crying out to God was my sanctuary. Even when I could not see Him, I felt His presence—small, quiet, but undeniable. Those prayers, those moments of surrender, were the threads holding me together when everything else threatened to unravel.

THE WAR IN MY HEAD

Mental warfare is real. And it's exhausting.

It's not always dramatic. It's not always loud. Sometimes, it's just a quiet voice in your head that whispers, *"You're not going to make it. You're not strong enough. Everyone would be better off without you."* Sometimes, it's waking up in the morning and feeling so heavy that getting out of bed feels impossible. Sometimes, it's going through the motions of life while feeling completely numb inside. Sometimes, it's smiling in public while screaming internally.

I've battled my mind for as long as I can remember. The thoughts come in waves—sometimes, small and manageable, sometimes, crashing over me with such force that I can barely breathe.

There were nights when I stood on the rooftop and stared down into the darkness, wondering what would happen if I just let go. Nights when I thought about ways to disappear, to make the pain stop, to finally rest.

What kept me here? I'm not always sure. Sometimes, it was fear. Sometimes, it was a small spark of hope. Sometimes, it was my grandmother/great-grandmother's prayers. Sometimes, it was God Himself, reaching down in those darkest moments and holding me, even when I couldn't feel Him.

THE BATTLE OF SILENCE

Silence was another battlefield. I wanted to scream, to let someone know how much I was hurting, but fear kept me quiet. Not being able to share the depth of your pain, feeling like no one would understand if you spoke out—these were heavy burdens.

I carried my struggles alone. Not because I wanted to, but because I didn't know who to trust. I didn't know who would understand. I didn't know who would use my vulnerability against me.

So I smiled in public and cried in private. I showed up to church and pretended everything was fine. I went to school and acted like I had it together.

But inside, I was falling apart.

The isolation was suffocating. It's one thing to fight battles when you have people standing with you. It's another thing entirely to fight them alone, in silence, with no one to witness your struggle or validate your pain.

The silent battles are often the hardest ones. Because when no one knows you're fighting, no one knows to pray for you, to check on you, to offer help. You're left to fight in isolation, and that isolation can become its own kind of prison.

THE REPETITIVE CYCLES THAT TRAPPED ME

What I didn't understand at the time was that the cycles weren't just habits—they were distractions.

They kept me focused on the immediate—what I was doing wrong, how I felt in the moment, whether I had failed again—instead of who I was becoming or where my life was going. I stayed caught in a loop of reacting instead of growing.

I would tell myself I was going to change. Be more disciplined. More consistent. More focused. And for a while, I was. I'd go to the gym. Eat better. Stay committed. I'd feel like I was finally gaining control.

But the pattern always repeated.

And the cycle would continue.

What made it dangerous wasn't just the behavior—it was how it kept me stuck. It pulled my attention away from the bigger picture and locked me into survival mode. I wasn't building a future. I was managing failure.

This was especially true in my struggle with lust. There were seasons where I felt strong—weeks, even months of walking in purity. I thought I had finally broken free. But when I fell, it felt like starting over from zero.

Sin. Shame. Repentance. Determination. Progress. And then—back again.

I felt like a hypocrite. How could I talk about God when I couldn't even get my own life together?

But I'm learning something crucial: Victory doesn't come through self-effort. It comes through the Holy Spirit- and understanding that changed everything. Because cycles like that don't just drain your strength- they distort your focus. They keep you looking at your failures instead of your purpose. They keep you busy surviving instead of moving forward.

THE HOLY SPIRIT'S ROLE IN BREAKING CYCLES

For years, I tried to break these cycles in my own strength. I'd make resolutions. I'd create plans. I'd try harder, do better, be more disciplined.

And I'd fail. Every single time.

Because here's the truth: **You cannot overcome sin in your own strength. You need the Holy Spirit.**

When the Holy Spirit assures you of something, and you choose to be obedient to that conviction, He gives you the power to walk it out. Not by willpower. Not by trying harder. But by His strength working in you.

Romans 8:13 says, *"For if you live according to the flesh, you will die; but if by the Spirit you put to death the misdeeds of the body, you will live."*

By the Spirit. Not by yourself. By the Spirit.

When I tried to stop watching porn by my own strength, I failed. But when I invite the Holy Spirit into that struggle, when I pray for His strength every time I'm tempted, when I obey His promptings to turn away—that's when I experience victory.

When I try to be consistent with the gym, healthy eating, or any other discipline in my own strength, I eventually burn out. But when I surrender it to God, when I ask Him to give me the strength and motivation I lack, when I do it as an act of worship rather than an act of willpower—that's when it becomes sustainable.

The pattern is the same for everything: **Obedience to the Holy Spirit, not self-effort, is what brings breakthrough.**

And that's freeing. Because it means I don't have to be strong enough. I just have to surrender enough. I don't have to have it all together. I just have to be willing to let God work in me.

Philippians 2:13 says, "For it is God who works in you to will and to act in order to fulfill his good purpose." God doesn't just call us to obedience—He gives us the desire and the ability to obey.

That's grace.

FIGHTING UNTIL YOU'RE TIRED

It's exhausting. Demoralizing. Soul-crushing.

It's the feeling of waking up every day and forcing yourself to keep going when every part of you wants to quit. It's crying out to God and hearing silence. It's doing everything right and still seeing no breakthrough. It's watching everyone else seem to succeed while you're still stuck in the same place.

There have been many days when I've thought, *I can't do this anymore. I don't have the strength. I'm done.*

But then I think about the fact that these seasons are God-designed and that there's always a lesson that needs to be learnt in that time.

Because, eventually, you will cross over. Eventually, the season ends. Eventually, you will enter new territory, new connections, new careers, your life partner, destiny helpers, and you will have a complete positive shift in your life.

Your wilderness season has an expiration date. You won't be here forever. The season may be long—it may feel unbearably long—but it will end. And when it does, when you finally cross over into your promised land, you'll understand why you had to go through what you went through.

THE ENEMY'S STRATEGY

I realized that the enemy attacks the mind because he knows that once he controls your thoughts, he controls your life. If he can convince you that you're worthless, you'll act like you're worthless. If he can convince you that things will never change, you'll stop fighting for change. If he can convince you that God has abandoned you, you'll abandon your faith.

The mind is the battlefield. And the enemy is strategic. He doesn't always attack with obvious temptations. Sometimes, he attacks with subtle lies that sound almost true.

"You're not good enough."

"You'll never overcome this."

"God is disappointed in you."

"You've messed up too many times."

"Everyone else has it together—you're the only one struggling."

These lies are designed to isolate you, to make you feel alone, to convince you that your situation is hopeless, that God is not real.

But 2 Corinthians 10:5 tells us to *take captive every thought to make it obedient to Christ.*

That means I have to fight back. I have to recognize the lies for what they are. I have to counter them with truth—God's truth.

When the enemy says, "You're worthless," I have to say, "I am fearfully and wonderfully made."

When he says, "You'll never change," I have to say, "I can do all things through Christ who strengthens me."

When he says, "God has given up on you," I have to say, "Nothing can separate me from the love of God."

This is spiritual warfare. And it's a daily fight. Sometimes, you have to handle things moment by moment. But the more I practice taking those thoughts captive, the better I get at recognizing the enemy's voice and rejecting his lies.

THE GRACE FOR TODAY

One of the most important lessons I've learned is that God gives grace for today. Not for tomorrow. Not for next week. For today.

When I look at all my problems at once—all the debt, all the struggles, all the battles—I feel overwhelmed. Crushed. Like there's no way forward.

But when I focus on just today, just this moment, it becomes manageable.

Do I have what I need for today? Yes.

Can I make it through today? Yes.

Is God with me today? Yes.

That's enough. That has to be enough.

Matthew 6:34 says, *"Therefore do not worry about tomorrow, for tomorrow will worry about itself. Each day has enough trouble of its own."*

I'm learning to live in the present. To trust God for today and let tomorrow take care of itself. To stop projecting all my fears into the future and instead focus on this moment, this day, this breath.

Because when I do that, when I narrow my focus to just today, I realize I've always had what I needed. I've always made it through. God has always provided. Maybe not in abundance, but always enough.

And if He's been faithful every day up until now, why would He stop being faithful today?

WHEN YOU FIGHT UNTIL THERE'S NOTHING LEFT

There's something powerful that happens when you fight until you're completely spent, until you're on the floor with nothing left—and you still choose to trust God.

That's when you discover that His strength really is made perfect in weakness. That's when you realize you were never meant to do this on your own. That's when you finally stop trying to be strong and let Him be strong for you.

I've been on that floor many times. Physically exhausted. Emotionally drained. Spiritually depleted. With nothing left to give, nothing left to fight with, nothing left but a whisper of faith that says, "God, if You don't come through, I'm done."

And every single time, He's come through. Maybe not in the way I expected. Maybe not in the timing I wanted. But He's come through.

He's kept me in my apartment when I had no money for rent. He's put food on my table when my bank account was empty. He's given me the strength to face another day when I thought I had none left. He's reminded me of His promises when I've forgotten them. He's sent people to encourage me at exactly the right moment.

2 Corinthians 12:9 says, "But he said to me, 'My grace is sufficient for you, for my power is made perfect in weakness.' Therefore, I will boast all the more gladly about my weaknesses, so that Christ's power may rest on me."

When I'm weak, He's strong. When I'm empty, He fills me. When I'm at the end of myself, He's just getting started.

THE HOPE THAT KEEPS YOU ALIVE

I've held onto hope even when I had no reason to. Even when my circumstances screamed that things would never change. Even when everyone around me had given up on me.

That hope wasn't based on my situation. It was based on God's character. On His promises. On His track record of faithfulness in my life.

And that hope has sustained me. It's kept me alive through seasons that should have killed me. It's kept me believing through circumstances that should have destroyed my faith.

Psalm 42:11 says, *"Why, my soul, are you downcast? Why so disturbed within me? Put your hope in God, for I will yet praise him, my Savior and my God."*

Even in the midst of mental battles, even when my soul is downcast, even when I'm disturbed and struggling—I put my hope in God. Because He's the only solid ground I have. The only foundation that won't crumble. The only constant in a world of variables.

And that hope? It won't disappoint. Romans 5:5 promises, "And hope does not put us to shame, because God's love has been poured out into our hearts through the Holy Spirit, who has been given to us."

THE BRIDGE FORWARD

The battles in my mind taught me that I couldn't survive on my own strength. That I needed God, not just as a concept, but as a living, active presence in my daily life.

But understanding that I needed God and actually experiencing His power were two different things. I needed to learn what it meant to walk in spiritual authority. To recognize that the struggles I was facing weren't just psychological or circumstantial—they were spiritual. The next layer of my journey was learning to fight not just with determination, but with divine strategy. To understand the seasons God was taking me through and why each one was necessary for my growth and ultimate release into purpose.

SCRIPTURE ANCHOR

"For if you live according to the flesh, you will die; but if by the Spirit you put to death the misdeeds of the body, you will live."

— Romans 8:13 (NIV)

"But he said to me, 'My grace is sufficient for you, for my power is made perfect in weakness.' Therefore, I will boast all the more gladly about my weaknesses, so that Christ's power may rest on me."

— 2 Corinthians 12:9 (NIV)

"Why, my soul, are you downcast? Why so disturbed within me? Put your hope in God, for I will yet praise him, my Savior and my God."

— Psalm 42:11 (NIV)

KEY LESSON

Mental battles are not signs of failure, but invitations to lean deeper into God's strength. Victory over repetitive cycles comes not through willpower but through surrender to the Holy Spirit. When you fight until you have nothing left and still choose to trust God, that's when His power is most evident. Hope anchored in God's character—not in your circumstances—sustains you through the darkest seasons. Each day carries its own grace; focus on today and trust God with tomorrow.

REFLECTION MOMENT

Pause and consider: What lies has the enemy been speaking over your life? What repetitive cycles have you been trying to break in your own strength, rather than through the Holy Spirit? When have you fought until you had nothing left—and how did God show up in that moment?

Write down one mental battle you're facing and one truth from God's Word you can use to fight back.

CHAPTER 10

SPIRITUAL WARFARE OF REFINEMENT

LIFE IS RARELY A STRAIGHT PATH. FOR ME, IT HAS ALWAYS BEEN A journey of seasons: **Removing** → **Separating** → **Preparing** → **Releasing.**

These phases are not random—they are intentional processes God uses to shape us, refine us, and prepare us for our destiny. But the enemy doesn't want us to see it that way.

Throughout each stage, I faced spiritual warfare. The enemy knew that if he could attack my mind, my heart, or my spirit, he could delay my purpose. He whispered doubt, fear, shame, and guilt. He tried to convince me that God had abandoned me, that I was unworthy, and that I would never make it, that I didn't have the money, that I was never going to do all these things I had in mind.

There were moments when I felt overwhelmed, hopeless, isolated, numb, drained, and like I was going crazy. Some days, I could not feel ANYTHING. I remember one night I cried so much I begged God, "Please do not let me wake up the next day. I don't want to be here." But still, I woke up alive the next day.

However, I've learned that if you are called to win souls or if an assignment has been placed on your life, we ain't going nowhere until they have come to pass. The enemy cannot kill what God wants alive. I've realized that God *does* care about how I feel, and He will refresh my spirit, remind me of His Word and who He is, and what He has called me to do on this earth.

But through it all, I learned the power of prayer, fasting, and Scripture. When I focused on Jesus, I discovered strength I didn't know I had. Spiritual warfare is not just about resisting temptation—it's about staying aligned with God's plan even when everything in your life seems chaotic. It's about holding on to faith when you can't see the full picture.

Hence, allowing God to fight your battles for you rather than moving ahead of what He is doing in that season. This has taught me the importance of being still and remembering that this life is not mine—it is God's—and I am on this earth as an agent for Him to carry out what He has planned for my life.

THE FOUR PHASES OF DIVINE REFINEMENT

God has a pattern. A process. And understanding that process has helped me make sense of seasons that otherwise felt senseless.

1. REMOVING

This is when God starts clearing out what is harmful—relationships, habits, or patterns that are not serving your purpose. It often feels painful because we resist letting go of what is familiar, even if it's toxic. But removal is necessary for growth.

I've experienced this removal in multiple ways. Friends who I thought would be with me forever suddenly drifted away. Jobs I thought were secure were taken from me. Opportunities I was sure were "God's will" closed without explanation.

At the time, it felt like loss. Like God was stripping me of everything I valued. Like He was punishing me rather than preparing me.

But now, looking back, I can see that he was removing what would have hindered me. People who would have held me back. Situations that would have kept me comfortable but stagnant. Relationships that were draining me rather than building me.

When I lost my job in August of 2025, it felt devastating at first. I was angry. Confused. Scared. But as time passed, I began to see that God was redirecting me. That job was never meant to be permanent. It was a season. God was removing it to make space for what He really called me to do—ministry, writing, business, and more.

Removal feels like loss in the moment. But it's actually protection. God is clearing space for what He's about to bring into your life. You can't carry new wine in old wineskins. Sometimes, God has to remove the old to make room for the new.

2. SEPARATING

During separation, God positions you away from distractions, negative influences, or environments that might pull you off course. This phase can feel lonely, but it is essential for clarity and focus.

Separation was one of the hardest seasons for me. I found myself increasingly isolated. Friends stopped calling. Invitations dried up. Everybody seemed distant.

I remember making the decision to take a break from social media. I announced it publicly, thinking people would understand. Instead, many got offended. They stopped talking to me. They made assumptions about why I was pulling back—some thought I was hiding from someone, others thought I was going through something scandalous or weird.

The truth was simpler: God told me to separate. To step back. To focus on what He was calling me to do, without the noise and distraction of everyone else's opinions and expectations.

Sometimes, God will silence the communication between you and a friend, which doesn't mean that person is not your friend anymore—it simply means God's preparation requires you alone. If God calls you into isolation, you must obey.

But that obedience cost me relationships. It cost me community. It left me feeling more alone than I'd ever felt. Even in certain moments when I refused to listen to God, He abruptly and gracefully destroyed relationships that I was holding on to. I remember driving home from church, weeping because it all felt so heavy, but deep down, I knew it was best.

In those moments, some people made comments that I was either doing the most, that I was being dramatic, or that I was trying to act holier than everyone else. But they didn't understand. They couldn't see what God was doing behind the scenes.

Separation isn't about making everyone else comfortable. It's about being obedient to what God is calling you to, even when no one understands.

Separation isn't punishment—it's preparation. God separates you so He can speak to you clearly, without the noise of other voices drowning out His direction. In the wilderness, away from the crowd, you learn to hear His voice distinctly.

Exodus 33:7 talks about how Moses would go to the tent of meeting, separate from the camp, to meet with God. Sometimes, you have to step away from everyone else to truly encounter God.

3. PREPARING

This is the season of the fire. The refining. The shaping. It's where your character is tested, your faith is stretched, and your endurance is built. You're being equipped for something bigger than you can see in the moment.

Preparation doesn't feel productive—it feels repetitive, exhausting, sometimes pointless. But every trial is part of His curriculum. Every hardship is sharpening you for the assignment ahead.

Right now, as I write this book, I'm in a season of preparation. I have no job. No income. Bills piling up. Rent unpaid for months. Debt collectors are calling. My car got repossessed. And yet, God is telling me to focus on this book, on my project, on ministry.

But God is preparing me. He's teaching me to trust Him when I can't see the way forward. He's teaching me to obey, even when obedience looks foolish. He's teaching me that His provision doesn't always look like what I expect.

This season is hard. Some days, my faith is strong. Other days, it's barely there. I wake up and wonder if today will be the day I get evicted. If today will be the day everything falls apart.

But it hasn't. And I believe it won't.

Because even in this wilderness, even in this season of lack, I feel God's presence. I hear Him saying, *"Trust Me. I've got you. Haven't I kept you this far?"*

And He has. Every single time, He has.

1 Peter 5:10 says, "And the God of all grace, who called you to his eternal glory in Christ, after you have suffered a little while, will himself restore you and make you strong, firm and steadfast." The suffering isn't wasted. It's part of the process that makes you strong, firm, and steadfast.

In Psalm 119:71, David says, "It was good for me to be afflicted so that I might learn your decrees." There's something you can only learn in the affliction. Something you can only discover in the fire.

4. RELEASING

Finally, God releases you into your purpose. What you have endured, what you learned, what you overcame—it all positions you to step boldly into your calling.

The enemy may still try to discourage you, but by this phase, you are stronger, wiser, and more prepared than ever.

I'm not fully in the release phase yet. I'm still in preparation. But I can feel it coming. I can sense that something is about to shift, that doors are about to open, that a breakthrough is near.

I can feel the season changing. Like when you're in winter, and you start to smell spring in the air. You can't see the flowers yet, but you know they're coming.

And when God finally releases me into the fullness of what He's called me to, I'll be ready. Not because I'm perfect, but because I've been through the fire and came out refined.

The book will be done. The project will be recorded. The ministry will be launched. And all the struggle, all the lack, all the waiting will make sense.

Release isn't just about doors opening. It's about walking through those doors with the character, wisdom, and spiritual maturity you gained in the previous seasons. God doesn't rush you into release. He waits until you're ready.

A TIME TO BE SILENT

There is a real season in life where the Lord will silence you.

Not because you've done something wrong—but because what He's doing in your life is too important to be disrupted by your own words.

If we're honest, our mouths can get ahead of our faith. We say what we feel, we speak what we fear, we confess doubt without even realizing it. And the truth is, unbelief has a voice. Negativity has a voice. Fear has a voice. And if those voices are loud enough, they can interfere with what God is trying to establish in your life.

That's why there are moments when God will quiet you.

Because if He doesn't, you might talk yourself out of the very thing He's working to bring to pass.

Your mouth is powerful. Scripture makes that clear over and over again. So when God is moving on your behalf—when He's working in the spirit to release something into the natural—He will sometimes guard that process by guarding you. By silencing you. By pulling you back from speaking too soon, too much, or to the wrong people.

There will be seasons where you notice it:

You're not as talkative as you used to be.

You don't feel the urge to explain everything.

You're more reserved with your words.

And you might wonder, *"What's going on with me?"*

What's happening is spiritual.

The Holy Spirit is teaching you restraint.

He's protecting the process.

He's shutting your mouth before your words can sabotage your promise.

Because God knows—if He lets you speak freely in certain seasons, you might disrupt what He's doing.

So He calls you into silence.

And if you resist that silence—if you keep talking when He's telling you to be still—there are times when He will enforce it. Just like He did with Zechariah, who was made unable to speak until God's word came to pass (Luke 1:20). Not out of cruelty, but out of purpose.

There is a time to speak. But there is also "a time to keep silent" (Ecclesiastes 3:7).

And you have to learn the difference.

Because not everything can be shared prematurely.

Not everything should be spoken out loud.

And not everyone is meant to hear what God is doing in your life.

Some people will mishandle it.

Some will doubt it.

Some will speak against it.

And if you're not careful, their voices will mix with yours—and before you know it, what God was building starts to feel uncertain.

So God says, *"Be quiet for a while."*

Not forever. Just for the season.

I had to learn this the hard way.

I learned that things started moving faster when I stopped talking so much.

I learned that God moved more freely when I wasn't constantly explaining, questioning, or announcing everything.

I learned that silence isn't punishment—it's protection.

So if you find yourself in a season where you're quieter than usual...

where you feel pulled back...

where you don't have much to say...

Don't fight it.

Lean into it.

Because that silence might be the very thing preserving what God is about to do in your life.

MONITORING SPIRIT

As we journey through life, we must learn to be honest with ourselves about the reality of the world around us.

Not every spirit carries peace.

Not every presence carries good intentions.

Some people enter your life with love, while others enter with hidden jealousy, silent competition, and unhealthy curiosity about your life.

This is why discernment is so important.

There are people who constantly watch your movements, monitor your progress, study your growth, and pay attention to every blessing unfolding in your life — yet remain silent about their own. They gather information but never pour back into you. They want access to your life without genuinely supporting your purpose.

Be careful of people who only appear when God begins elevating you.

Be careful of people who celebrate you publicly but secretly resent you privately.

Be careful of people who are uncomfortable with your growth because your progress reminds them of their own stagnation.

Not everyone around you is assigned to go where God is taking you.

Some individuals are attached to the old version of you. They are comfortable with the broken, struggling, limited version of your life because that is where they first encountered you. Your healing intimidates them. Your discipline bothers them. Your elevation exposes what they refused to confront within themselves.

And instead of growing with you, some people quietly hope for your downfall.

This is why you must guard your spirit, protect your peace, and pay attention to the energy surrounding your life.

Everybody smiling with you is not happy for you.

Everybody checking on you is not checking with pure intentions.

And everybody in your circle should not have unlimited access to your personal life.

Pray for discernment.

Pray for wisdom.

Pray for spiritual protection.

Especially during seasons where God is developing you, blessing you, and preparing you for greater things. The closer you get to purpose, the more important it becomes to evaluate the people connected to you.

Check your circle.

Check the conversations.

Check the motives.

Check the patterns.

Because some people do not want to see you evolve. They would rather keep you in the same place where they first met you — doubting yourself, struggling, and unable to grow beyond their comfort level.

But God did not create you to stay stuck.

Sometimes separation is protection.

Sometimes distance is necessary.

And sometimes God will reveal people to you slowly so you can finally see what your heart kept trying to ignore.

Protect your spirit at all costs.

Not everybody deserves access to the version of you that God is building.

THE ENEMY'S STRATEGY IN EACH SEASON

The enemy doesn't attack randomly. He's strategic. And his strategy changes depending on which season you're in.

In the Removing Season, he tries to make you hold onto what God is removing. He whispers, "You can't do this without them. You need that job. You'll never find another friend like that." He wants you to cling to what's being taken so you miss what's being prepared.

In the Separating Season, he attacks with loneliness and fear. He tells you that you're being punished, that God has abandoned you, that everyone has forgotten about you. He wants you to believe the isolation is permanent, rather than purposeful.

In the Preparing Season, he attacks with doubt and discouragement. He reminds you of your failures, your weaknesses, your past. He makes you question whether you heard God correctly. He tries to convince you to give up before the breakthrough comes.

I've experienced this so many times. In the middle of this current season, the enemy whispers constantly:

"You heard God wrong. This isn't His plan. You're just irresponsible. You should've taken that job offer. You're going to end up homeless. You're a failure."

But I've learned to recognize his voice. And I've learned to counter it with truth.

In the Releasing Season, he attacks with distraction and false opportunities. He tries to get you to settle for less than what God has for you, to take shortcuts, to step into something prematurely because you're tired of waiting.

When you understand the enemy's strategy, you can fight more effectively. You can recognize his voice and reject his lies. You can press through the discomfort of each season knowing that it's all part of God's plan.

Ephesians 6:12 reminds us, "For our struggle is not against flesh and blood, but against the rulers, against the authorities, against the powers of this dark world and against the spiritual forces of evil in the heavenly realms." This isn't just a mental battle. It's spiritual warfare. And it requires spiritual weapons.

PATIENCE: THE HARDEST LESSON

If there's one thing every season has taught me, it's patience. I'm not naturally patient. I want things to happen now. I want a breakthrough today. I want to see the fruit of my labor immediately.

But God's timing is rarely my timing. And learning to trust His timing—to truly trust it, not just say I trust it—has been one of the hardest lessons of my life.

Patience isn't passive. It's not sitting around doing nothing while you wait. It's active trust. It's continuing to do the work God has given you while you wait for Him to open the next door. It's staying faithful in the hidden season, knowing that what you do in private will be rewarded publicly.

Right now, I'm writing this book even though I don't have money for groceries. I'm recording my prayer CD even though I can't pay my bills. I'm preparing for my ministry even though I don't know when or where the doors will open. We have to know that, in these times, movement and action are a necessity. You are not allowed to just sit and do nothing; you must start working on that vision.

That's active patience. That's obedient waiting.

Isaiah 64:4 says, *"Since ancient times no one has heard, no ear has perceived, no eye has seen any God besides you, who acts on behalf of those who wait for him."*

God acts on behalf of those who wait. Not those who rush. Not those who try to force things. But those who wait.

And waiting doesn't mean being idle. It means being obedient in the season you're in, even when you can't see what's next.

I'm learning to wait well. To trust that God's delays are not denials. That His silence doesn't mean absence. That His timing is perfect, even when it doesn't feel like it.

Habakkuk 2:3 says, "For the revelation awaits an appointed time; it speaks of the end and will not prove false. Though it linger, wait for it; it will certainly come and will not delay."

The promise is coming. The breakthrough is coming. The release is coming. It will not delay beyond God's appointed time.

THE COST OF DISOBEDIENCE

I've learned the hard way that when God calls you to something, delayed obedience is still disobedience.

There have been times when God told me to do something—to let go of a relationship, to step away from an opportunity, to move in a certain direction—and I hesitated. I questioned. I delayed.

And every time I did, I suffered longer than I needed to. The season stretched out. The pain intensified. The lesson I was supposed to learn took longer to sink in.

But the moment I surrendered and obeyed—even when it was hard, even when it didn't make sense—God moved. Doors opened. Provision came. Peace returned.

I think about Jonah. God told him to go to Nineveh. He ran in the opposite direction. And what happened? He ended up in the belly of a fish for three days. His disobedience didn't change God's plan—it just delayed it and made his journey more difficult.

When he finally obeyed, when he finally went to Nineveh, God did exactly what He said He would do. The city repented. Lives were saved. Purpose was fulfilled.

But Jonah could have avoided the fish if he'd just obeyed the first time.

Romans 6:16 reminds us that whatever we yield ourselves to becomes our master. If you yield to fear, fear runs your life. If you yield to comfort, comfort keeps you stuck. But if you yield to God, His blessing flows.

Obedience unlocks the next level. Disobedience keeps you circling the same mountain. I don't want to circle anymore. I want to cross over. And crossing over requires obedience, even when it costs me.

RECOGNIZING THE SEASON YOU'RE IN

One of the most important questions you can ask yourself is: **What season am I in right now?** Because when you know what season you're in, you can respond appropriately. You can stop fighting what God is doing and start cooperating with it.

If you're in a Removing Season, let go. Stop clinging to what God is taking. Trust that He's making room for something better.

If you're in a Separating Season, embrace the solitude. Use it to draw closer to God, to hear His voice, to get clarity on what He's calling you to.

If you're in a Preparing Season, endure. Keep showing up. Keep doing the work. Keep trusting that this season has a purpose, even when you can't see it yet.

If you're in a Releasing Season, step out in faith. Don't shrink back. Don't play small. Walk boldly into what God has prepared for you.

For me, right now, I'm in the Preparing Season and transitioning toward Release. I can feel it. Approval. Congratulations. Increase. Abundance. The calling is becoming clearer. I'm not there yet, but I'm closer than I've ever been.

And I'm choosing to stay patient, to stay obedient, to stay faithful—even when it's hard, even when I'm tired, even when I don't understand everything. PLEASE DO THE SAME!

THE PROMISE FOR THOSE WHO ENDURE

James 1:12 says, *"Blessed is the one who perseveres under trial because, having stood the test, that person will receive the crown of life that the Lord has promised to those who love him."*

There's a crown waiting. A reward. Not just in eternity, but here on earth.

For those who endure the Removing season without becoming bitter. For those who endure the Separating season without losing faith. For those who endure the Preparing season without giving up. For those who step boldly into the Releasing season without fear.

There's a crown. A blessing. A fulfillment of purpose that makes every moment of struggle worth it.

I'm holding onto that promise. In the moments when I want to quit, when I'm tired, when I don't understand what God is doing—I'm holding onto the promise that there's a crown waiting for those who persevere.

And I'm determined to receive it.

Galatians 6:9 says, "Let us not become weary in doing good, for at the proper time we will reap a harvest if we do not give up." Don't give up. Your harvest is coming. Your breakthrough is near. Your release is closer than you think.

THE BRIDGE FORWARD

Understanding these seasons—Removing, Separating, Preparing, Releasing—gave me a framework to make sense of my life. But there was still one more layer I needed to understand.

Because the battles I faced weren't just personal. They weren't just about me overcoming my struggles and stepping into my purpose.

They were generational.

There were patterns in my family—cycles of pain, dysfunction, and bondage—that had been passed down for generations. And God was calling me to be the one who broke them.

The next phase of my journey wasn't just about my own freedom. It was about breaking chains that had held my family captive for decades.

SCRIPTURE ANCHOR

"Since ancient times no one has heard, no ear has perceived, no eye has seen any God besides you, who acts on behalf of those who wait for him."

— ISAIAH 64:4 (NIV)

"Blessed is the one who perseveres under trial because, having stood the test, that person will receive the crown of life that the Lord has promised to those who love him."

— JAMES 1:12 (NIV)

"Let us not become weary in doing good, for at the proper time we will reap a harvest if we do not give up."

— Galatians 6:9 (NIV)

KEY LESSON

Spiritual warfare tests every part of us, but it also teaches us to depend on God fully. Understanding the four seasons—Removing, Separating, Preparing, and Releasing—helps you cooperate with God's process rather than fight against it. Patience is not passive waiting; it's active obedience in the season you're in. Delayed obedience is still disobedience, and it prolongs your wilderness. The key is to recognize which season you're in and respond accordingly, trusting that God's timing is perfect, even when it doesn't feel like it.

REFLECTION MOMENT

Pause and reflect: What season are you in right now—Removing, Separating, Preparing, or Releasing? How might God be using this season to refine you and prepare you for what's next? Where have you been resisting God's process instead of cooperating with it?

Write down one area where you need to practice active patience, and one step of obedience you can take today.

CHAPTER 11

BLOODLINES & CURSE BREAKING

Sometimes, the battles we fight aren't just ours—they're battles passed down through generations.

We inherit more than eye color, height, or family traditions. We can also inherit cycles of pain, dysfunction, and patterns that look like they never want to let go. Abuse, addiction, poverty, broken relationships, sickness, inconsistency, identity struggles—it can all feel like a shadow following us, a script we didn't write but somehow keep performing.

I didn't always have language for it, but what I was experiencing was generational curses. These are patterns that don't just "happen," but seem to repeat themselves in families. At first, I thought it was just life, that maybe I was unlucky, or maybe I wasn't good enough. But as I grew in God, I began to see that what I was fighting wasn't random. It was spiritual.

THE PATTERN I COULDN'T IGNORE

As I got older and began to understand my family's history, I started noticing patterns. Things that repeated themselves across generations.

Broken marriages. Relationships that started with promise but ended in violence or abandonment.

Financial struggle. No matter how hard people worked, there was always lack, always debt, always just barely getting by.

Addiction. Alcohol was a constant presence in my family. My mother drank. My cousins drank. And it wasn't social drinking—it was destructive, daily, desperate drinking.

Anger and violence. The way conflict was handled in my family was always explosive, always physical, always leaving scars—both visible and invisible.

Inconsistency. People would start things and never finish them. Dreams would be abandoned. Potential would be wasted. A pattern of almost, but not quite.

Health issues. Cancer. Diabetes. High blood pressure caused the most deaths in my family, and sickness continued to repeat itself from generation to generation.

At first, I thought these were just individual choices, personal failures. But the more I looked, the more I realized: This wasn't just about my mother or father. This wasn't just about me. This was a family pattern. Something that had been repeating itself through generations—quietly, consistently, destructively. A cycle that had been running through my bloodline for decades, maybe longer.

And then I began to understand something deeper- it wasn't just something I was meant to recognize, it was something I was called to break.

UNDERSTANDING MY MOTHER'S STORY

For years, I struggled to understand why my mother treated me the way she did. Why was she so cruel? Why did she seem to hate me when I was just a child who wanted to be loved?

But as I got older, pieces of her story began to emerge. And slowly, painfully, I began to understand.

My mother lost her father when she was young. He died unexpectedly, and that loss shaped her in ways she probably never processed or healed from. She grew up without the stability, protection, and guidance a father provides.

There were whispers—things I heard from family members, things that were said in hushed tones but never fully explained. Whispers that my mother was never this way when she was younger.

When she was 18, she left Kingston, Jamaica, and moved to St. Mary, the countryside. That's when things began to shift—and not in small ways, but drastically. She started acting differently: cursing more, fighting more, drinking heavily.

It was like watching someone slowly become unrecognizable.

During that time, the tension between her and my dad grew worse. They fought every day—constant, exhausting conflict—until one day, without warning, he decided he couldn't take it anymore and left.

After that, things became even more unstable. She would get money and give it away just as quickly—buying things for other people, spending without hesitation or planning, without ever really considering her own needs, or the needs of her children.

Many people would question, "Is something wrong with her?" Because no normal person would do such a thing.

But it goes deeper than the natural eyes can see.

My mom has always carried herself in a very masculine way—in her walk, her talk, her demeanor. People called her the "Don of the Lane" because she fought like a man, cursed like a man, and commanded fear like a man.

She often wore men's clothing and rarely dressed in typical women's attire unless she was going to court—which was frequent, because she was often in and out of jail. Even outside of that, her presentation, her energy, her presence was overwhelmingly masculine. She would even take my clothes and wear them as I got older, which blurred the lines of individuality in ways I didn't fully understand at the time.

And I often wonder—though I can never fully know—if something in me reflected back to her in a way that unsettled her. My gentleness. My sensitivity. The parts of me that didn't match what she was. Maybe she saw herself in me. Maybe she resented what she had to suppress. Or maybe my existence reminded her of something she had buried so deeply she could no longer face it.

And as I've gotten older, I've begun to recognize something uncomfortable: I see some of her struggles in myself too—nconsistency, lack of discipline. Patterns that feel inherited, not just learned.

THE FIRE THAT CHANGED EVERYTHING

On December 7th, 2001, our house burned down.

The fire started in my great-grandmother's room—from a candle. It spread quickly, consuming everything in its path. The house was made of board, not concrete, and it offered almost no resistance.

My mother was the first to notice. I can still imagine her reaction—panic turning into a cry for help as she realized what was happening.

My little sister was inside at the time, lying on the bed while the fire began to intensify. In the chaos, my mother managed to get to her and pull her out.

But by then, it was already too late.

We lost everything.

After that night, we scattered—searching for places to stay, trying to find shelter wherever we could. We moved from place to place, sleeping wherever there was space, trying to rebuild a sense of normal life from nothing.

And even now, in 2025, we are still rebuilding.

That fire marked a turning point. It broke something in her. And the years that followed brought more struggle, more chaos, more spiritual warfare than I think any of us could fully comprehend at the time.

That doesn't excuse what she did to me. It doesn't make the abuse okay. But it helps me understand that her cruelty wasn't really about me. It was about her own unhealed pain, her own unresolved trauma, her own war with herself and people.

THE GENERATIONAL PATTERN OF HARDSHIP

As I began to piece together my family history, I started to notice a pattern—cycles of lack, unfinished beginnings, and things that never seemed to fully stabilize or last.

It wasn't just my mother and me. It ran through both sides of my family.

I began to see how many people around me were aware of what was happening, yet didn't fully understand why these patterns kept repeating—or what it would take to break them.

For me, that awareness pushed me deeper into prayer and faith, believing that if anything was going to change, it would have to be brought before God completely.

Because when patterns like these are left unaddressed, they don't just disappear—they repeat. They move from one generation to the next.

And I found myself thinking: I don't want this to continue through me.

This stops here.

I found the pattern. Clear, undeniable, running through our bloodline.

At first, I felt shame in that realization—like it meant something was inherently wrong with us. Like maybe the things people said about my family were true.

But over time, my understanding began to shift.

This wasn't permanent. It wasn't identity. It was a pattern.

And patterns can be broken.

Galatians 3:13 says, *"Christ redeemed us from the curse of the law by becoming a curse for us, for it is written: 'Cursed is everyone who is hung on a pole.'"*

Jesus already broke every curse on the cross. But somebody in the family line has to stand in the gap and activate that freedom. Somebody has to say, "Enough. This ends with me."

And God chose me to be that somebody.

WHY ME? THE WEIGHT OF BEING CHOSEN

Let me be honest—being chosen to break generational curses is heavy. Being chosen to bind and lose is heavy. It feels unfair. It feels exhausting.

I didn't ask for this. I didn't volunteer. I didn't raise my hand and say, "Pick me, God. Let me be the one who carries the weight of generations on my shoulders."

But God looked at me and said, *"I trust you to break it."*

And I'll admit, there were moments—many moments—when I didn't feel chosen. I felt punished. I felt like God was asking too much. I felt like I was suffering for sins I didn't commit, carrying shame that wasn't mine to carry.

Why did I have to be the one to go through all this abuse? Why did I have to be the one to face rejection from my community? Why did I have to be the one to wrestle with everything, while everyone around me seemed to have it figured out?

But slowly, I began to understand: **God doesn't choose the comfortable ones. He chooses the ones strong enough to carry the weight of a breakthrough.**

1 Corinthians 10:13 says, *"God is faithful; he will not let you be tempted beyond what you can bear."*

Sometimes, that verse isn't just about temptation—it's about the weight of calling. God looked at me and knew I could bear it. Not because I was naturally strong, but because He would give me His strength. Not because I had it all together, but because He would hold me together.

The devil doesn't attack what isn't a threat. If hell has its eyes on you, it's because heaven has already marked you as dangerous.

You are a threat. Your obedience, your prayers, your persistence—it terrifies the enemy because it means generations after you won't suffer the same battles you did.

HOW THE ENEMY ATTACKS THE CURSE BREAKER

When you're chosen to break curses, the attacks hit differently. For me, it came from every direction—family, friends, even strangers. I faced criticism, financial hardship, and rejection. People nitpicked everything I did. My very identity was under attack. Doubt and disbelief tried to creep in. My gift was tested. My peace was stolen.

And yet, the more I pressed into God, the more I realized: **Every attack revealed where the curse had its grip.**

If I was being hit in my finances, that's where the enemy didn't want me free. If I was being attacked in my mind, it was because clarity and purpose were on the other side. If relationships were strained, it was because unity was part of my assignment.

The enemy was showing his hand. And I learned to use his attacks as a roadmap—wherever he fought hardest was exactly where I needed to press in with prayer, fasting, and obedience.

MY MOTHER'S CONTINUED STRUGGLE

My mother is still alive. And she's still struggling.

She still drinks heavily. She still gets into fights with neighbors, family members, and random people. She still curses my younger siblings. She was even arrested recently and spent three days in jail for a gang war incident.

People in the community call the police on her regularly. She's still known as the "Don of the Lane," still feared, still volatile, still trapped in the same cycles she's been in for decades.

And it breaks my heart.

Because I see now that she's not just a cruel woman who chose to hurt me. She's a broken woman who never got help. A woman who carries trauma she never healed from. A woman who's under spiritual attack and doesn't even realize it.

When I confronted her about a year ago—when I finally had the courage to tell her how much her abuse affected me, how I still have nightmares about her beating me, how her words still echo in my head—she didn't have much to say.

She didn't apologize. She didn't try to explain. She didn't deny it or defend herself. She just went quiet.

And in that moment, I realized: She probably doesn't even fully understand why she did what she did.

Hurt people hurt people. And my mother? She's been hurting for a long, long time.

That doesn't make what she did okay. But it does make forgiveness possible.

BITTERNESS THAT POISONS

Some of us have difficulties letting go of things in the past, and because of this, are unable to move forward.

Ephesians 4:31–32 says, *"Get rid of all bitterness, rage and anger, brawling and slander, along with every form of malice. Be kind and compassionate to one another, forgiving each other, just as in Christ God forgave you."*

Never let a situation take power over your emotions, your peace, your future. I forgive because I've been forgiven. I extend grace because I've received grace. Not because it's easy, but because it's necessary.

And here's what I've discovered: When you forgive the people who hurt you most, you take away their power. They no longer control your emotions. They no longer dictate your peace. You're free. But forgiveness doesn't always mean access. Many people struggle with the question: should I let that person back into my life after what they did to me? And the truth is, while forgiveness is necessary, restoration requires more.

You can forgive someone and still choose to keep your distance. Because if that person hasn't changed- if they haven't addressed what caused the relationship to break in the first place- then they're likely to repeat the same behavior.

Healing requires growth. And if there's no change, the same cycle will repeat itself. So it's important to be discerning. Forgive freely, but be wise about who you allow back into your space.

HOW TO BECOME FINANCIALLY FREE

For a long time, I thought financial stability would just come with time—that if I worked hard enough, things would eventually fall into place.

But life showed me something different.

I've experienced what it feels like to go without—to not have enough, to struggle, to feel like no matter how hard you try, you're still behind.

And in those moments, I began to realize that financial freedom doesn't happen by accident. It requires growth.

What God began to show me is this: if I wanted my situation to change, I had to become more valuable.

Not just in what I do—but in who I am.

I started to understand that value is what creates opportunity. When you carry something that can help others—when you can solve problems, create, build, or contribute in a meaningful way—people begin to notice. Doors begin to open.

For a long time, I believed that just working a regular job would be enough. And while a job can provide stability, I realized it wasn't enough on its own to take me where I wanted to go.

There was more in me.

And I had to ask myself: *What has God placed inside of me that I haven't fully developed yet?*

That question changed everything.

Because when you begin to identify your gifts—your skills, your ideas, your purpose—and actually develop them, you begin to shift. You stop just working for money, and you start creating value.

And value attracts opportunity.

I'm still on that journey. Still learning. Still growing. But I now understand that financial freedom isn't just about how much you make—it's about who you become.

There is something in you that can open doors a job alone cannot. Something that can set you apart.

The key is to find it, develop it, and trust God enough to step into it.

BREAKING THE CURSE: PRACTICAL STEPS

Breaking generational curses isn't just about saying one prayer and everything vanishing overnight. It's a process. It's spiritual warfare. It requires persistence, fasting, and faith.

Here are the steps God taught me:

1. RECOGNITION

You cannot break what you will not name. Look at your family honestly. What patterns keep repeating? Addiction? Divorce? Poverty? Anger? Health issues? Financial lack? Call it out for what it is.

2. CONFESSION AND REPENTANCE

Bring those patterns to God. Confess not only what was done to you, but any ways you may have contributed to continuing the cycle. Ask for His forgiveness and His power to break free.

3. DECLARE FREEDOM

Speak life over yourself and your bloodline. Say out loud: *"This curse ends with me. My children will not carry this. My grandchildren will not suffer this."*

Use Scripture as your weapon. Stand on Galatians 3:13. Stand on Numbers 23:23, which says, *"There is no divination against Jacob, no evil omens against Israel."*

4. TAKE PRACTICAL STEPS

Prayer is powerful, but you must also walk differently. Break habits. Set boundaries. Pursue education. Get counseling or therapy if needed. Choose differently from those before you. Align your actions with your prayers.

5. PERSEVERE

The fight will not be easy. There will be resistance. The enemy doesn't give up territory without a fight. But curses break under consistent pressure. Keep pressing. Keep fasting. Keep declaring freedom.

For me, this looked like getting therapy to process the trauma. It looked like choosing not to drink alcohol, even though it was normalized in my family. It looked like setting boundaries with family members who tried to pull me back into dysfunction. It looked like pursuing education even when resources were scarce. It looked like choosing obedience to God over comfort.

THE COST AND THE REWARD

Breaking generational curses has cost me. It's cost me relationships with family members who don't understand. It's cost me the comfort of fitting in. It's cost me years of struggle, of feeling alone, of carrying weight that, sometimes, felt unbearable.

But the reward? The reward is freedom. Freedom for me. Freedom for my future children. Freedom for generations that come after me.

They won't have to fight the same battles I fought. Exodus 20:5–6 says that God punishes the children for the sin of the parents to the third and fourth generation of those who hate Him, *"but show[s] love to a thousand generations of those who love me and keep my commandments."*

One generation of obedience can unlock blessings for a thousand generations. One person choosing to break the cycle can change the trajectory of an entire family line.

That's the power of being a curse breaker. You're not just changing your life—you're changing your family's future.

A WORD TO OTHER CURSE BREAKERS

If you're reading this and you recognize yourself in my story—if you see generational patterns in your family that need to be broken—I want you to know something:

You are not alone. And you are not crazy.

The weight you feel is real. The spiritual warfare is real. The resistance from family members who don't understand is real.

But so is your calling. So is God's power. So is the breakthrough that's coming. Don't give up. Don't back down. Don't let the enemy convince you that the curse is too strong to break.

Jesus already broke it on the cross. You're just activating what He already did. Stand in the gap. Pray the prayers. Make the declarations. Take the practical steps. And watch God move.

Your obedience today is paving the way for generations tomorrow. Your children will grow up in freedom because you chose to fight. Your grandchildren will inherit the blessing because you refused to pass on the curse.

That's legacy. That's purpose. That's what it means to be chosen.

THE BRIDGE FORWARD

Breaking generational curses taught me that my life wasn't just about me. My story wasn't just about my survival. It was about setting captives free—starting with my own family, but extending far beyond.

But there was still one more crucial lesson I needed to learn before I could fully step into my calling. I needed to understand that the God I served wasn't confined to the four walls of a church building. That a true relationship with Him wasn't about religious performance—it was about genuine encounters.

The next phase of my journey would take me away from the institution and into the wilderness, where I would finally meet God for myself, beyond the noise of religion and into the reality of relationship.

SCRIPTURE ANCHOR

"Christ redeemed us from the curse of the law by becoming a curse for us, for it is written: 'Cursed is everyone who is hung on a pole.'"
— GALATIANS 3:13 (NIV)

"Get rid of all bitterness, rage and anger, brawling and slander, along with every form of malice. Be kind and compassionate to one another, forgiving each other, just as in Christ God forgave you."

— EPHESIANS 4:31–32 (NIV)

"I, the Lord your God, am a jealous God, punishing the children for the sin of the parents to the third and fourth generation of those who hate me, but showing love to a thousand generations of those who love me and keep my commandments."

— EXODUS 20:5–6 (NIV)

KEY LESSON

Your legacy is not predetermined. You do not have to repeat what your parents or grandparents did. In Christ, you are empowered to break destructive cycles, walk in freedom, and create a new story for yourself and the generations after you. The fight may be heavy, but the victory is guaranteed. Being a curse breaker is costly, but the reward—freedom for a thousand generations—is worth every battle. Forgiveness doesn't excuse the harm done; it releases you from being controlled by it.

REFLECTION MOMENT

Pause and reflect: What patterns have you noticed repeating in your family? Where in your life do you feel resistance the strongest—finances, relationships, health, identity, or consistency? How can you begin declaring freedom and taking practical steps today? What areas of obedience is God calling you into right now that could unlock freedom for your family line?

Write down one generational pattern you're committed to breaking, and one action step you'll take this week.

CHAPTER 12

FINDING GOD BEYOND THE PEWS

There was a season in my life when I felt utterly disillusioned with the church.

I had grown up immersed in religion, surrounded by familiar rituals and customs. My grandmother and great-grandmother raised me in the church. Sunday services were routine. Prayer meetings were expected. Fasting was mandatory.

Church was simply what we did. Yet I began to see that being in church did not always equate to experiencing God. Some of the people I trusted the most—those who were supposed to nurture my faith—lied, gossiped, and even tried to suppress the calling God had placed on my life.

It hurt deeply. I felt betrayed, frustrated, and even angry at God.

WHEN CHURCH PEOPLE HURT YOU

The church was supposed to be my refuge. A place where I could escape the abuse at home, the bullying at school, the rejection in my community. A place where I'd finally be safe, accepted, loved.

But it wasn't.

The same people who lifted their hands in worship on Sunday were the ones spreading gossip about me during the week. The same people who shouted "Amen" during the sermon were the ones whispering, saying something in the parking lot.

I shared things with people I thought were safe—people I called brothers and sisters in Christ. I opened up about my struggles, my pain, my questions. And those very things I shared in confidence became ammunition used against me.

They told others. They twisted my words. They used my vulnerability to create narratives that weren't true. And when I confronted some of them, they justified it as "concern".

But gossip is gossip, even when you dress it up in religious language.

Church—the place that should have been my sanctuary—became another battlefield.

That betrayal cut deeper than the abuse at home or the bullying at school. Because I had learned to expect those places to be hostile. But I expected the church to be different. I expected Christians to act like Christ. And when they didn't, it shattered something inside me.

THE MOMENT I WALKED AWAY

There came a point when I couldn't take it anymore. I stopped going to church. Not just for a week or two, but for an extended season. I walked away from the institution, from the people, from the routine I'd known my entire life.

People had opinions about that, too. They said I was backsliding.

They said I was rebellious. They said I was letting the devil win. But the truth was simpler: I was tired. Tired of performing. Tired of pretending. Tired of being judged by people who claimed to follow a God of grace, but showed none themselves.

I needed space. I needed to figure out who God was to me, not who the church said He was. I needed to separate the institution from the relationship.

And so I left.

During that time, I did things I'm not proud of. I sinned. I wandered. I made choices that contradicted everything I'd been taught. I numbed my pain in ways that only created more pain.

I was angry—at the church, at God, at myself. I felt abandoned. If God was real, if He really loved me, why did He allow His people to hurt me like this?

But here's what I learned: God never left me, even when I left the church. His presence followed me into my wandering. His voice still spoke to me in my rebellion. His love still held me, even when I was running away from Him.

MEETING GOD IN THE WILDERNESS

It was during that time away from the church—during COVID, in 2020—that I actually encountered God in the deepest way I'd ever experienced.

Not in a church service. Not during a praise and worship set. Not through a sermon. But in my room, alone, crying out to Him in desperation.

I remember the moment I was refilled with the Holy Spirit. It wasn't dramatic. There were no church lights, no music, no altar call. It was just God and me.

I was at my lowest. Broken. Empty. And I cried out, "God, if You're real, I need You to show me. Not what the church says You are. Not what the Bible study leader says You are. I need to know who You are to me."

And He showed up.

I felt His presence in a way I'd never felt before. Not as a distant deity who demanded perfection, but as a Father who loved me in my mess. Not as a God who was disappointed in me, but as a Savior who was pursuing me even in my rebellion.

He began to reveal things to me. He opened my eyes to see people for who they really were—both the ones who genuinely loved me and the ones who were against me. He gave me discernment I'd never had before. He started speaking to me directly, personally, intimately.

That's when I realized: Faith is not about the people or the institution. It's about a personal relationship with God. And you can't borrow someone else's relationship with Him. You have to find Him for yourself.

WHAT I LEARNED ABOUT RELIGION VS. RELATIONSHIP

Walking away from the church taught me the difference between religion and relationship.

Religion is about performance. It's about showing up, saying the right things, following the rules, and looking holy in front of others. It's external. It's exhausting. And it's empty.

Relationship is about intimacy. It's about being honest with God—even when you're angry, even when you're struggling, even when you don't have it all together. It's internal. It's genuine. And it's life-giving.

Religion asks, "What do I have to do to be accepted by God?"

Relationship says, "I'm already accepted by God. Now, how do I walk with Him?"

Religion focuses on behavior modification. Relationship focuses on heart transformation.

Religion makes you feel like you're never good enough. Relationship reminds you that Jesus is good enough on your behalf.

I grew up in religion. But during my time away from the church, I found relationship.

And once you experience a real relationship with God, you can never go back to just religion. You can never settle for the performance. You crave His presence.

THE CHURCH HURT THAT LED TO ISOLATION

Even after I came back to God, I struggled with going back to church. I'd been hurt too deeply. I'd seen too much hypocrisy. I'd experienced too much betrayal from people who claimed to represent Christ.

So I isolated myself. I worshiped alone. I prayed alone. I studied the Word alone. I convinced myself I didn't need community, that I could have a relationship with God without being part of a church family.

And for a season, that worked. God met me in my isolation. He spoke to me in my solitude. He showed me things I wouldn't have seen if I'd been surrounded by noise.

But over time, I realized something: **Isolation was never God's permanent plan for me.**

God created us for community. Not a toxic community that wounds you, but a healthy one that builds you up. Not a religious community that judges you, but a grace-filled one that walks alongside you.

During a recent three-day fast, God spoke to me clearly about this. He said, *"Community is important. You can't do what I'm calling you to do alone. You need people. The place I'm taking you requires a team, requires support, requires relationships built on genuine love and trust."*

I'd been avoiding the community because I was afraid of being hurt again. But God was calling me to risk again, to trust again, to open my heart again—this time with discernment, with boundaries, but also with hope.

Hebrews 10:25 says, "Let us not give up meeting together, as some are in the habit of doing, but let us encourage one another—and all the more as you see the Day approaching." We need each other. Not church as a building or an institution, but church as a body of believers genuinely committed to each other.

REDEFINING WHAT CHURCH MEANS

I'm learning to redefine what church means to me.

Church isn't just a Sunday service. It's not just a building I go to once a week. It's not about titles, positions, or looking spiritual in front of others.

Church is wherever believers gather in authentic community. It's the group of friends who pray for me when I'm struggling. It's the mentor who speaks truth into my life. It's the people who show up when I need help, not because they have to, but because they genuinely care.

Church is less about the institution and more about the relationships. Less about the performance and more about the presence of God.

I still attend services when I can. But I'm more selective now. I look for places where grace is extended, where brokenness is acknowledged, where people are real rather than pretending to be perfect.

And I'm learning that it's okay to have boundaries with church. It's okay to protect my peace. It's okay to walk away from environments that are toxic, even if they're labeled "Christian."

God doesn't require you to stay in places that wound you. He doesn't ask you to subject yourself to spiritual abuse in the name of commitment. Sometimes, leaving is the most spiritually mature thing you can do.

THE CALLING I COULDN'T ESCAPE

Even during my time away from the church, even during my season of wandering, there was a calling on my life I couldn't escape.

Ministry. Preaching. Leading others to Christ.

I tried to ignore it. I tried to convince myself that someone as broken as me, someone who'd struggled with so much, couldn't possibly be used by God in that way. But the calling wouldn't go away. It followed me. It pressed on me. It whispered to me in quiet moments, reminding me that God had marked me for something greater than my pain.

I remember the first time I preached. I was nervous, unsure, convinced I would mess it up. But when I opened my mouth and began to speak, something shifted. The words flowed. The anointing was tangible. People responded—not to me, but to the God speaking through me.

And I realized: **God doesn't call the qualified. He qualifies the called.**

My brokenness didn't disqualify me. My struggles didn't make me unworthy. My past didn't determine my future. God was going to use every bit of my pain, every moment of my suffering, every lesson I'd learned in the wilderness—and turn it into a message that would set others free.

2 Corinthians 1:4 says that God "comforts us in all our troubles, so that we can comfort those in any trouble with the comfort we ourselves receive from God." Your pain is not wasted. It becomes the platform for your purpose.

WAITING ON GOD

Waiting on God is one of the hardest seasons a person can go through. You're told to trust Him, to have faith, to believe that His plan is already laid out—even when you can't see how anything will come together.

The truth is, waiting isn't hard because we're incapable of patience.

It's hard because of the weight of what we're carrying while we wait.

The suffering can feel unbearable. The silence can feel endless. For some, it brings deep sadness, anxiety, or even depression. There are moments when you truly can't see a way out—especially when you feel like you have no one to turn to.

Sometimes, it's just you and God.

And even then, the waiting doesn't always make sense.

But what I've come to understand is this: God doesn't move you into the next season until both you *and* that season are ready. Even when it looks like everything is in place… it may not be prepared for you yet. And you may not be prepared for it.

That's the tension.

Because when a new season is close, you can feel it. You can sense the shift. It looks like it's right there—within reach. And yet, you're still waiting.

In those moments, it's easy to grow restless. To get distracted. To try to force your way into something that isn't fully ready.

But timing matters.

Because stepping into something too early—before you're ready, before it's ready—can cost you more than the wait ever would.

So even when it's hard, even when it stretches you beyond what feels manageable, there is purpose in the delay.

Psalm 13:1–2 captures this feeling perfectly: *"How long, Lord? Will you forget me forever? How long will you hide your face from me? How long must I wrestle with my thoughts and day after day have sorrow in my heart?"* But the psalm ends with trust: *"But I trust in your unfailing love; my heart rejoices in your salvation."*

Even when I can't feel God, I choose to trust His character. Even when I can't hear Him, I choose to believe His promises. Even when He feels distant, I choose to remember that He's never once failed me.

THE LUKEWARM SEASON I BATTLED

If I'm being honest, there was a season when my faith felt lukewarm.

I wasn't on fire for God. I wasn't deeply in sin. I was just... existing. Going through the motions. Praying occasionally. Reading my Bible when I felt like it. Showing up to church out of habit, rather than hunger.

I was comfortable. Complacent. Content with mediocrity.

And God wasn't okay with that.

Revelation 3:16 says, *"So, because you are lukewarm—neither hot nor cold—I am about to spit you out of my mouth."*

That verse terrified me. Because I realized that's where I was. Lukewarm. And God was shaking me, assuring me, refusing to let me stay in that place.

He began to stir something in me again. A hunger. A desperation. A longing for more than just casual Christianity.

And that stirring led me here—to writing this book, to stepping into ministry, to pursuing the calling He placed on my life with everything I have.

God doesn't want casual followers. He wants sold-out believers. He wants people who are all in, not halfway loyal. And sometimes, He has to shake up our comfortable lives to get us to that place of full surrender.

THE BRIDGE FORWARD

Finding God outside the walls of the church changed everything. It gave me a foundation that wasn't dependent on people's opinions or religious performance. It gave me a relationship with Him that was real, raw, and unshakeable.

But understanding who God was to me was only part of the journey. I still had to learn how to walk with Him through the impossible.

Because the next season would test my faith like never before. I would have to trust God's provision when I had nothing. I would have to believe His promises when circumstances screamed otherwise. I would have to step into calling without knowing how it would all work out.

The wilderness was about to become my classroom. And the lessons I learned there would prepare me for everything God had planned next.

SCRIPTURE ANCHOR

"Let us not give up meeting together, as some are in the habit of doing, but let us encourage one another—and all the more as you see the Day approaching."

— HEBREWS 10:25 (NIV)

"[God] comforts us in all our troubles, so that we can comfort those in any trouble with the comfort we ourselves receive from God."

— 2 CORINTHIANS 1:4 (NIV)

"So, because you are lukewarm—neither hot nor cold—I am about to spit you out of my mouth."

— REVELATION 3:16 (NIV)

KEY LESSON

God's presence is not limited to religious institutions—faith is deeply personal. Hurt from church people does not mean God has abandoned you; it means imperfect people have failed to reflect His perfect love.

Walking away from toxic environments, even Christian ones, is sometimes necessary for spiritual health. Your relationship with God is about intimacy and honesty, not performance and perfection. Community is important, but it must be a healthy, grace-filled community built on genuine love. Your calling doesn't disappear because you wander; God pursues you even in your rebellion.

Pause and reflect: How has your faith been shaped by your personal relationship with God, apart from church or others' influence? Have you been hurt by church people, and if so, how has that affected your view of God? In what ways can you deepen your connection with Him in solitude and stillness? Where might God be calling you back into a healthy community, even if you've been wounded before?

Write down one step you can take to pursue an authentic relationship with God beyond religious performance.

CHAPTER 13

Crossing Over While Under Fire

Moving to America for my master's degree was a dream I had carried since I was in undergrad. I prayed for it, worked toward it, and when it finally began to become real, I was grateful—so grateful. But getting here and staying here was not the fairy tale I had imagined. The road was dangerous, messy, and at times, I wondered whether I would even survive long enough to see the classroom doors open.

THREE MONTHS BEFORE DEPARTURE: THE ROBBERY

Three months before I was set to leave Jamaica for graduate school, I was robbed.

It wasn't just theft. It was violent. Terrifying. And it could have ended my life.

After work one evening, I was waiting for a cab to head home. One pulled up—just a driver inside. I didn't think much of it. I got in, not knowing my life was about to hang in the balance.

A few minutes into the drive, something felt off. The driver said he needed to make a quick stop to pick something up. My heart began to race. I tried to stay calm, but panic was creeping in.

He drove to an unfamiliar location.

When we stopped, I saw them.

Men.

They surrounded the car.

One got into the front seat. Another shifted near the trunk. Then someone slid in beside me in the back.

At that moment, I knew.

The man in front turned and grabbed my backpack. Then I felt it—a cold piece of metal pressed against my head.

Everything changed.

They took everything. My phone. My wallet. My belongings. All of it.

They told me if I stayed calm, they wouldn't hurt me. So I sat there, trying to breathe, praying silently.

Then one of them said,

"When we stop the car, be quiet and run—or else."

Moments later, they pushed me out.

I fell into a gully—a deep, dark ravine.

For a second, everything went still.

Then instinct took over.

I ran.

I didn't look back.

In my mind, I cried out,

God, if this is it, please be with me. But if You're not done with me yet, please save me.

And the Lord said,

"The devil can't kill what I want alive."

They didn't shoot.

To this day, I don't fully understand why.

I climbed out, shaken, disoriented, trying to steady myself. I walked back to the road, forcing my body to stay calm even though everything inside me was screaming.

I kept saying one thing:

I need to get home.

A woman passed by. I stopped her, my voice trembling, and told her what had happened. She gave me $100 JMD—just enough to get me partway.

When that ran out, I found a schoolmate at a bus stop who paid the rest without hesitation.

When I finally got home, I sat in silence.

I was supposed to be preparing for America—for a new chapter, a new beginning.

Instead, I was trying to process how close I had come to losing my life.

But God kept me.

I should have died that day.

He wasn't done with me yet.

THE VISA DENIAL

As if the robbery wasn't enough, when I went to the U.S. embassy to apply for my student visa, I was denied.

The consular officer reviewed my financial statement and told me I didn't have enough funds to cover tuition and living expenses—even though I had the exact amount listed on my I-20. They advised me to secure a scholarship and reapply.

I left the embassy devastated.

I had been accepted to Nova Southeastern University. I had a plan. I had worked and saved every dollar from my summer job for this moment.

But now, because of money—the very thing I had struggled with my whole life—the door seemed to be closing.

I didn't know what to do. I didn't have a backup plan.

So I prayed.

And I placed it in God's hands.

Then, somehow, things began to shift.

I received a scholarship.

I gathered my documents and reapplied, holding on to faith even as uncertainty tried to take over. Every day, I checked the visa portal, hoping for an update.

Waiting.

Believing.

And this time, my visa was approved.

For a moment, I felt relief.

I thought the worst was behind me.

I thought I could finally breathe.

I thought I could finally prepare to leave.

But the attacks weren't over.

THE IRON TO THE HEAD

A week before I was supposed to travel, my landlord's nephew—who, I later learned, was struggling with mental health issues and had missed his medication—broke into my room.

I was lying on my bed on my stomach, about to sleep, when the door was suddenly forced open with aggression. Before I could react, he struck me in the head with a heavy metal iron.

I fought back instinctively, screaming for my housemate Pete, who came running when he heard the noise. The intruder fled.

I didn't even realize I was bleeding until I slammed the door shut and saw the red smear against the white paint. I touched my head— blood was running down my face, onto the bed, and onto the floor.

Panic hit me. I honestly thought I was going to die.

My friend called the police, and when they arrived, they took me straight to the hospital.

Fifteen stitches. A tetanus injection. And a kind of trauma that went far beyond the physical wound.

Afterward, I went to the police station, but nothing came of it. "Mental health issues," they said. Not much they could do. The landlord said the same. I was left to process it on my own.

What shook me most was learning, just days later, that the same man had attacked an elderly neighbor—and killed him.

In that moment, something settled in me: I had been spared.

I couldn't stay in that house anymore. I spent a few nights with a friend before traveling home to St. Mary to recover.

On the morning I left, my mother and her friends came for me. On the way, I felt a strong sense that something was wrong with the car. I asked them to stop.

When we got out, we saw that both back tires were completely flat. On a dark road at night, we could have gone off the edge without knowing.

I stood there in the dark and prayed—grateful for a warning I almost ignored.

Looking back, I know I should have died—or at the very least been severely harmed. But I wasn't.

I was kept.

FINALLY ARRIVING IN AMERICA

When I finally stepped off the plane in Miami, I was traumatized.

The robbery. The visa denial. The gun to my head. The blown tires. All of it weighed on me as I landed on new soil.

I arrived with just enough money to pay for my first semester—and nothing more. No plan for what came next. No safety net. No apartment lined up.

I landed on faith.

I sat in the airport for hours, trying to figure out my next move. Then I remembered my friend's mother, Cheryl Swaby, who lived nearby.

I called her and explained my situation.

She didn't hesitate.

She welcomed me in.

The next day, she and her mother drove me around until we found a place close to campus that I could afford. The night before I moved in, they packed boxes of food, toiletries—everything they thought I might need.

When we loaded it into the car, I broke down.

Just days before, I had no idea how I was going to survive. And now, God had already gone ahead of me—placing someone in position to help me before I even arrived.

But the challenges didn't stop there.

After my first semester, I had a hold on my account and needed money for summer classes. Even in that moment, I was determined to finish my degree in less than two years—despite everything.

My academic advisor stepped in and helped clear the hold.

Later, when I needed a graduate assistantship, a connection through the International Affairs Office led me to an opportunity with Campus Life and Student Engagement.

I did the interview outside, in the middle of summer heat—sweating, distracted, surrounded by noise. It wasn't ideal. It wasn't polished.

But I showed up.

And I got the position.

That role became more than just a job—it became a place where God began rebuilding my confidence.

I was guided by my supervisor, Tamara, and my director, Gerard. And I was supported by people—Lilian, Monique, Shekinah, and Hailey—who became like family.

When I had no ride to campus, they showed up.

When I felt low, they encouraged me.

When I didn't have food, they shared what they had.

When I questioned whether I belonged, they reminded me of who I was.

Even in the unknown, God had already placed provision, favor, and community exactly where I needed it.

"Being confident of this, that he who began a good work in you will carry it on to completion until the day of Christ Jesus." — Philippians 1:6

If He starts something in you, He will finish it.

THE THREAT OF HOMELESSNESS

After graduating, I faced another crisis. I had only days to pack and vacate my apartment, and I had nowhere to go. I reached out to friends and ended up staying with one, then with my cousin, for months while I waited for my work authorization documents to be approved by USCIS.

Six months of unemployment. Six months of sending out applications, doing interviews, and hearing nothing back while waiting for my approval.

Then, one morning, I checked the USCIS portal and saw the word I wasn't expecting: denied.

Sadness and confusion barely described it. My school explained what I needed to do—resubmit, pay another $500 fee, wait another two months. I was back at square one, extending my stay with people who had already been more than generous. I felt like a burden, even if they never made me feel that way. My heart just needed everything to work out now.

The atmosphere grew heavy. Mentally, I started suffering. I had no choice but to turn to the only thing I knew could sustain my mind. I cried every day, fasted every day, and prayed every day.

There were moments where morning and evening walks became a thing for me just because it freed my mind. Some days, I'd sit from 8 a.m. to 12 a.m., till my butt hurt, because somehow I felt like if I stopped pressing, my breakthrough would not come.

I was exhausted.

But even in that exhaustion, something in me refused to give up.

I didn't have answers.

I didn't have stability.

But I still had faith.

And sometimes, that was the only thing holding me together.

JOB OFFERS

Until the day everything shifted.

Two job offers landed almost at the same time—one a remote position based in Florida, the other a teaching role in New York. On paper, it looked like opportunity. In reality, I had nothing—zero dollars in my account and no clear way to get to either place.

Still, somehow, I made it to Florida.

Even now, I can't fully explain it. I just know I showed up for a three-day training with more faith than resources, holding on to the quiet belief that if I took one step, something—or Someone—would meet me there.

One evening after training, everyone casually gathered their things and walked out to the parking lot, keys in hand, engines starting one by one. I followed the crowd, but when they reached their cars, I stopped.

Because I didn't have one.

No ride. No backup plan. Just me, standing there, trying not to panic.

So I prayed.

It wasn't a long, polished prayer—just something honest, something desperate. And then I felt it: a small, steady nudge. *Try booking an Uber.*

It didn't make sense. I had no money. But I opened the app anyway, half-expecting it to fail.

It didn't.

The ride went through.

I remember staring at my phone in disbelief, as if it might suddenly correct itself. But it didn't. The car arrived. I got in. And in that quiet moment, I realized: I wasn't doing this alone.

By the time training ended, I was still standing at a crossroads—Florida felt safe, predictable. New York felt like risk, like exposure. Like stepping out onto something that might not hold me.

That's when I met my friend for dinner.

I told her everything—the fear, the uncertainty, the constant mental back-and-forth. She listened, really listened, and then looked at me with a kind of certainty I didn't yet have for myself.

"You should go," she said. "Don't limit yourself. You never know what can happen."

It wasn't a long speech. It didn't need to be.

Something in me clicked.

A week out from leaving, I went all in on New York—with nothing but determination and an empty bank account. I scrolled through Facebook Marketplace, messaging strangers, asking about subleases I had no guarantee I could afford.

Most conversations went nowhere.

Except one.

There was a man who kept responding—consistent, patient. And two days before I was supposed to leave, he offered me his room. Not just that—he explained that he worked nights and would find somewhere else to stay on his days off so I could have the space.

I remember sitting there, staring at the message, stunned.

Why would someone do that for me?

A friend's mother stepped in and lent me the $350 deposit. Another door opened. Another provision I couldn't have arranged on my own.

And when I moved out three months later, that same man handed me back $500.

Not what I gave him—more.

He told me God had placed it on his heart.

In that moment, I didn't just feel helped—I felt *seen*.

I worked both jobs for a while after that. Long days, longer nights. But slowly, things began to change. I bought my first car. I moved into my first apartment—with a credit score that, by most standards, shouldn't have qualified me for anything.

Still, I got in.

My whole life, I had been used to figuring things out alone—no safety net, no steady support system. Just me, pushing forward, piece by piece.

But looking back, I can see it clearly now:

I was never actually alone.

God had been with me in every closed door, every last-minute provision, every moment where things should have fallen apart—but didn't.

And I've learned something in all of this—Miracles don't just happen out of nowhere.

They meet you in motion.

There is something sacred about the decision to move, even when you don't have all the answers. Because staying still produces nothing, but when you act, when you step forward in faith, you make room for the miraculous to meet you there.

THE MOMENT AT THE TRAIN STATION

There was a season when I sat at a train station for hours, bags of clothes beside me, my phone charging from an outlet on the floor. I had no money. I didn't know where to go next. I couldn't afford a ticket any-where—and honestly, I didn't know where I would sleep that night.

I sat there confused, exhausted, and quietly weeping.

God, this cannot be my life.

I have been nothing but faithful.

I am only 25 years old.

The weight of it all pressed in on me as the hours passed.

Then, out of nowhere, my cousin sent me money, and I went to stay with her again—for a while.

But even then, I felt abandoned. Unwanted. Like a burden no one wanted to carry.

Still, I prayed.

I kept praying—asking God to make a way where there seemed to be none.

And this is what that moment taught me:

There is no situation too heavy, too unclear, or too far gone for God to step into.

Even if it's at the last second. Even if it comes in a way that doesn't make sense at all.

So stay alert. Stay open. Stay in expectation.

Because something will break. Something will shift. Something will change.

THE SPIRITUAL ATTACK ON MY SIGHT

During this same season of instability, I went through one of the most terrifying spiritual attacks I have ever experienced. I woke up one evening and couldn't see. My vision was blurred and distorted. I was so dizzy that every time I tried to stand, I felt like I was falling. I thought I just needed water—I drank some, but nothing changed.

I went to a doctor. They gave me medication, but I didn't improve. Two days later, things were worse. A second hospital said they needed to transfer me by ambulance to a facility with better equipment, because I could neither see clearly nor walk without stumbling. They ran every test. They kept me overnight. Everything came back normal. No one could tell me what was wrong.

That night in the hospital bed, I had a dream: I was standing in a dark, abandoned place—completely surrounded by wolves charging toward me from every direction. But every time they came close, they couldn't touch me. Arrows were sent.

They couldn't touch me either. I understood the dream when I woke up: the enemy had deployed everything against me, and none of it could break the covering over my life.

I prayed harder. I fasted. I declared healing over my body. I renounced every assignment sent against me. And God healed me—slowly, the vision returned, the dizziness faded. The doctors never found a cause. But I knew. It was a spiritual attack on my sight—not just my physical eyes, but my ability to see where God was taking me. The enemy was trying to disorient me, to make me lose my way at the moment I was closest to crossing over.

It is so important that we understand the difference between a spiritual attack and spiritual preparation—because when we can't identify which one we're facing, we approach the season in the wrong way and end up defeated, fighting the wrong thing.

"So we fix our eyes not on what is seen, but on what is unseen, since what is seen is temporary, but what is unseen is eternal." — 2 Corinthians 4:18

The very enemy who tried to break me, blind me, and leave me homeless was defeated. God restored me tenfold. What I lost in one season was multiplied in the next.

LESSONS FROM THE FIRE

Looking back on everything that happened—the robbery, the visa denial, the attack with the iron, the near-homelessness, the spiritual attack on my sight—I can see God's hand in all of it. The enemy tried to stop me from getting to America. He tried to kill me, blind me, and leave me without resources or support. He threw everything he had at me.

But he failed.

Because God's purpose for my life is bigger than the enemy's plans against it. Here is what I learned from crossing over while under fire:

1. The enemy fights hardest when a breakthrough is near. If hell is coming after you with everything it has, it's because heaven has already marked you for something significant. The intensity of the attack is often proportional to the significance of the assignment.

2. God's provision doesn't always look like abundance—sometimes, it looks like just enough, given at exactly the right time. I didn't have excess. I didn't have a cushion. But every time I needed something, God provided exactly what I needed, exactly when I needed it.

3. Storms don't last forever. It felt like one attack after another, like the trials would never end. But they did. The season shifted. And on the other side of the storm, there was my breakthrough.

4. What the enemy means for evil, God turns for good. Every attack I faced was meant to destroy me. But God used each one to strengthen me, to teach me to depend on Him, to prepare me for what was coming next.

"And we know that in all things God works for the good of those who love him, who have been called according to his purpose." — Romans 8:28

If you're reading this and you're in the middle of your own "crossing over" season—where it feels like everything is falling apart just as you're trying to step into something new—I want you to know: this is not the end. This is the transition.

The enemy attacks transitions. He attacks people who are about to cross over into their promised land. But if you're under attack, it means you're moving in the right direction. It means the enemy sees something in you that he's afraid of. It means breakthrough is close. Don't give up.

Don't turn back. Don't let the intensity of the battle convince you that you're on the wrong path.

Keep moving. Keep trusting. Keep declaring that God is faithful and His promises are true.

Wherever you go. Even through the robbery. Even through the attack. Even through the wilderness of uncertainty. God is with you. And He will bring you through.

"Have I not commanded you? Be strong and courageous. Do not be afraid; do not be discouraged, for the Lord your God will be with you wherever you go." — Joshua 1:9

THE BRIDGE FORWARD

Crossing over while under fire taught me that God's faithfulness isn't just a comforting concept—it's a lived reality. He doesn't just promise to be with us; He shows up in the darkest, most desperate moments and makes a way where there is none.

But making it to America, finishing graduate school, getting a job, a car, and an apartment—that wasn't the finish line. It was only the beginning. Because the real work was never about geographical location or educational achievement. The real work was about stepping fully into the calling God had placed on my life—walking in the authority He had given me, using my voice, my story, and my testimony to set others free.

The final season was here. The season of release. And everything I had endured was preparing me for this moment.

SCRIPTURE ANCHOR

"Being confident of this, that he who began a good work in you will carry it on to completion until the day of Christ Jesus."

— PHILIPPIANS 1:6 (NIV)

"And we know that in all things God works for the good of those who love him, who have been called according to his purpose."

— Romans 8:28 (NIV)

"Have I not commanded you? Be strong and courageous. Do not be afraid; do not be discouraged, for the Lord your God will be with you wherever you go."

— Joshua 1:9 (NIV)

KEY LESSON

The enemy fights hardest when your breakthrough is near. Attacks during transition are not signs that you're on the wrong path—they are confirmation that you're moving in the right direction. God's provision may not look like abundance, but it always comes exactly when you need it. Storms are temporary, but the character and faith you develop inside them are permanent. Miracles happen when action meets activation. What the enemy means for evil, God will always turn for good.

REFLECTION MOMENT

Pause and reflect: What "crossing over" season are you in right now? What attacks or obstacles have you faced that might actually be confirmation you're headed toward a breakthrough? How has God provided for you in unexpected ways during difficult transitions?

Write down one storm you're currently facing, and declare God's faithfulness over it, trusting that this season will pass and your breakthrough is near.

____

____

____

____

____

____

____

____

____

____

____

____

____

____

____

CHAPTER 14

THE PARENT I NEVER ASKED TO BE

Growing up, I was the parent I never asked to be. From the time I was in primary school—before I even fully understood what the word "responsibility" meant—I was taking care of my four younger siblings.

Cleaning diapers. Washing and folding clothes. Clipping nails, washing hair, bathing little ones, cooking meals, staying up through the night when babies cried, and picking them up from school.

Everything a parent should do, I was doing it. All of it.

My mother went out late—most nights she didn't come back until five in the morning, if she came back at all. Their father was not in the picture. So it fell to me. I was the father. I was the mother. I was whatever they needed me to be, even on the nights when I had nothing left.

THE WEIGHT OF RESPONSIBILITY

Everybody in my community knew. They saw it. I was the one running the household while my mother was at the bar drinking and smoking. I didn't know the first thing about raising children—but I had to learn, and fast, because they needed *someone*. If it wasn't me, it was nobody.

There were nights with no baby formula in the house. I'd make sugar and water to keep the babies calm because it was all we had. But even so, I refused to do nothing.

Growing up, I had always been drawn to elderly people—I'd stop on the street to help them carry their bags or hold their hands, and over time, those same people would press a little cash into my hand: "Go buy yourself something to eat." I took that money and bought Lasco—a Jamaican powdered milk—to feed the babies instead. It was not enough, but I used what I had.

Even now, I still take care of my siblings where I can—sending money when I have it, calling to encourage them, guiding them. They're not little anymore, but they're still mine in my heart. I believe I am paving the way for them so that half of what I experienced, they will not have to face. And once God blesses me fully, I will pour everything I have into them. They are one of the reasons I push as hard as I do—because it's not only for me. It's for the greater good. It's for them.

But I never asked for any of it. I never asked to be a parent at seven, eight, nine, or ten years old. I never volunteered to carry that weight. At the end of the day, though, I had to. And I did.

THE NIGHTS I DIDN'T SLEEP

There were countless nights when I couldn't sleep—not because I didn't want to, but because my siblings needed me. A baby crying at 2 a.m. needed to be fed. A toddler who wet the bed needed to be changed. A scared child needed to be comforted. And my mother? She wasn't there.

I remember rocking babies to sleep when I should have been sleeping myself. I remember waking early to make sure everyone was fed, bathed, and ready for school before I ever thought about getting myself ready. I remember the exhaustion—the bone-deep tiredness that came from being responsible for lives that were never mine to be responsible for. If I said no or pushed back, I would get cursed out or hit for being disrespectful. Every day felt like slavery.

My childhood was stolen from me. Not just by the abuse I endured personally, but by the responsibility that was forced on me before I was old enough to understand what I was carrying. I didn't get to play. I didn't get to be carefree. I didn't get to just be a kid. I had to be a parent.

THE GUILT I STILL CARRY

Even now, as I write this, I feel guilt. Guilt that I'm not there with them. Guilt that I'm in America, pursuing my dreams, while they're still back in Jamaica, navigating my mother's unpredictability and the absence of a father. Guilt that I escaped, and they haven't yet.

I know it's not my responsibility to save them. I know I did everything I could when I was there. I still help them when I can. But the guilt is still there—because I know what that house feels like from the inside. I know what it means to deal with her rage, her neglect, her cruelty. My younger brother, who is only fifteen, is already trying to find ways to leave. My twelve-year-old sister is acting out. I know why. The environment is toxic for a child's development, and it leaves marks.

Once, I received a distressing phone call—they were hungry. They hadn't eaten all day. And at that moment, I had nothing to send. I couldn't eat myself after that call, knowing they were going without. In that moment of helplessness, I brought it to God. And He said to me: "Do not worry about them. They will be just fine. Just like I took care of you, I will do the same for them. Focus on yourself for now, and I will take care of them."

A level of peace settled over me that I can't fully explain, but I chose to trust it.

What I know is this: Parents, please take the time to nurture your children rather than neglect them. Children should be treated with the same respect that is required of them. Neglect creates trauma that follows children into adulthood and shapes decisions they'll make long after they leave your house, and if you are the oldest sibling who is always providing, start focusing on you.

THE LESSONS I LEARNED FROM RAISING THEM

Raising my siblings taught me things I never would have learned any other way. It taught me patience. When you're up in the middle of the night with a crying baby or a child who can't understand why their mother isn't home, you learn patience quickly—or you break. I chose patience.

It taught me sacrifice. There were many times I went without so *they* could have. Times I didn't eat so they could eat. Times I put their needs ahead of mine without thinking twice.

It taught me unconditional love. Even when I was exhausted, even when I was overwhelmed, even when I wanted to give up—I loved them. They were innocent in all of this. They didn't ask to be born into this situation any more than I did. And they deserved to be loved, cared for, and protected.

It taught me responsibility in the deepest sense—not the kind you choose, but the kind you accept because someone has to. Sometimes, you carry weight that isn't yours because no one else will. And sometimes, carrying it anyway is exactly what love looks like.

And it taught me that family isn't always about blood. It's about who shows up. It's about who stays. I showed up for my siblings every single day, even when I was barely surviving myself.

THE COST OF BEING THE ELDEST

Being the eldest came with a cost I didn't fully understand when I was young, but feel deeply now.

I didn't get to depend on anyone. I had to be the dependable one. I had to be the strong one. I had to hold it together—even when I was falling apart inside. I couldn't have my own bad days without worrying about how they would affect the little ones around me. If I was hurting, I still had to be their comfort. If I was scared, I still had to be their protector.

I became the parent, the provider, the protector—all roles I wasn't equipped for, but had to fill anyway. And even now, at twenty-seven, I struggle with asking for help because I'm so used to being the one others lean on. I struggle with letting people take care of me because I spent my entire childhood taking care of everyone else. That's the cost. And it's a cost I'm still processing.

MY PRAYER FOR THEM

Every day, I pray for my siblings.

I pray that God protects them. That He shields them from the worst of my mother's behavior. That He sends people into their lives who will love them and guide them in ways she cannot.

I pray that they don't internalize her words the way I did. That they don't believe the lies she tells them about their worth or their future.

I pray that they break free sooner than I did. That they find safety, stability, and peace before the damage goes too deep.

I pray that the cycle ends with me—that the generational curses I am breaking don't get passed down to them. That they grow up knowing they are loved and worthy, not because of what they do, but because of who they are.

"A father to the fatherless, a defender of widows, is God in his holy dwelling." — Psalm 68:5

My siblings may not have had the parents they deserved. But they have a God who sees them, loves them, and will defend them. And they have me—imperfect, still healing, but here. Always here.

THE VOW I MADE TO MYSELF

I made a vow when I was still young and raising my siblings: I will never treat my own children the way I was treated.

I will never make them feel like burdens. I will never use my words as weapons against them. I will never abandon them emotionally, even if I am physically present. I will never ask them to raise one another because I'm too consumed by my own pain to parent them properly.

I will break every cycle. I will create a new legacy. And I will make sure my siblings know that no matter what happens, no matter how far away I am, they have someone in their corner who believes in them—someone who will fight for them, someone who sees their worth even when the world has tried to convince them otherwise.

That's my vow. That's my commitment. That's my legacy.

A WORD ABOUT INTERCEDING FOR YOUR FAMILY

Something I've learned on this journey is that asking God for forgiveness is not only for yourself—it's for your family too. Many of the battles we fight are rooted in things our family did before us, patterns of sin and brokenness that we didn't create but are still living inside of. God is just, and nothing escapes His notice. When those who came before us fail to repent, the weight of those patterns can press on those who come after them.

This is not about God punishing the innocent. It's about how generational patterns—spiritual, emotional, behavioral—carry forward until someone breaks them through prayer, repentance, and obedience. Carrying the weight of your family's healing is never easy. But it is worth it.

Begin praying for your family line. Ask God to forgive what they didn't know to confess. Stand in the gap. The warfare may be intense, but you are not fighting alone.

BLEEDING WHILE LEADING

There are seasons in life where you still have to show up while silently falling apart inside.

You still have responsibilities.

People still depend on you.

Bills still have to be paid.

Commitments still have to be honored.

And somehow, even while carrying pain that nobody can fully see, you are expected to keep moving.

Some of us know what it feels like to pour into others while running on empty ourselves. To encourage people while secretly battling discouragement. To wear a smile in public while privately fighting battles that leave us mentally exhausted.

There are moments when life feels overwhelming — like you are drowning beneath the deepest part of the ocean with no way back to the surface. Moments where you sit in silence, staring out of a window at trees moving in the wind, feeling completely disconnected from everything around you.

Blank.

Numb.

Confused.

Emotionally exhausted.

Not because you do not care, but because internally, you are bleeding.

The hardest part is that most people will never fully understand what you are carrying. They may see your strength, but they cannot always see your suffering. And when pain goes unseen for too long, it can begin to feel even heavier.

But this is the reality for many people during certain seasons of life.

The goal is not to pretend the pain does not exist.

The goal is not perfection.

The goal is simply not to give up.

Even when the pressure becomes unbearable.

Even when your mind is tired.

Even when your heart feels worn down by life.

Why?

Because if you give up now, you may never see what God was doing behind the scenes the entire time.

Sometimes God works in silence.

Sometimes He builds us in hidden places.

Sometimes the season that feels like it is breaking you is actually the season that is transforming you.

You may feel forgotten, but you are not abandoned.

Every hardship, every sacrifice, every silent tear — God sees it all. Nothing you have endured has gone unnoticed.

And one day, the pain that nearly broke you will become proof that you survived.

People will see your growth.

You will see your growth.

And most importantly, you will realize that God never left your side.

So if you are bleeding while leading, keep going.

This season will not last forever.

And it will get better.

THE BRIDGE FORWARD

Raising my siblings taught me that love is a choice. Not a feeling that comes and goes, but a daily decision to show up, to sacrifice, to put someone else's needs before your own.

And that understanding—that deep, lived-in understanding of sacrificial love—prepared me directly for the calling God placed on my life. Because ministry is the same. Preaching is the same. Writing this book is the same. It's choosing to show up for people, even when it costs you.

It's choosing to pour out, even when you're running on empty. I learned that on the nights I rocked my siblings to sleep. I learned it on the mornings I made sure they ate before I did. I learned it in the hundreds of small, unseen moments when I chose them over myself.

Now, God is asking me to make that same choice on a larger scale—to pour out for people I've never met, to sacrifice for the Kingdom, to love sacrificially not just my siblings but everyone who will read this book, hear my upcoming projects, and sit under my preaching.

The training ground was my childhood. The mission field is the world.

And I am ready.

SCRIPTURE ANCHOR

"A father to the fatherless, a defender of widows, is God in his holy dwelling."
— Psalm 68:5 (NIV)

"Greater love has no one than this: to lay down one's life for one's friends."
— John 15:13 (NIV)

KEY LESSON

Sometimes, God calls us to carry weight we never asked for. That weight can feel unbearable in the moment, but it shapes us, strengthens us, and prepares us for the calling ahead. The sacrifices we make—even the ones that feel deeply unfair—are never wasted. They become the foundation of our testimony and the training ground for our purpose. Breaking cycles isn't just about our own freedom; it's about ensuring the next generation doesn't have to fight the same battles we did.

REFLECTION MOMENT

Pause and reflect: What responsibilities have you carried that were never yours to carry? How have those experiences shaped who you are today? What cycles are you committed to breaking so the next generation doesn't inherit your pain?

Write down one way you can use the sacrifices you've made to bless someone else, and one prayer you can pray for the people you've had to take care of.

RELEASED INTO PURPOSE

Looking back over the seasons of my life, I can see how every trial, every heartbreak, and every moment of pain was intentional.

God never wasted a single struggle. Each season—whether it was **Removing, Separating, Preparing**, or **Releasing**—was designed to shape me, strengthen me, and guide me toward the purpose He had for my life.

I remember the nights of isolation, the feelings of worthlessness, and the moments when I doubted if I would ever make it. I remember walking through abuse, betrayal, rejection, and spiritual warfare. And yet, here I am.

Not just because of my own strength, but because God faithfully orchestrated every step of the journey.

THE SEASONS THAT SHAPED ME

The Removing Season stripped away everything I thought I needed. Friends who I thought would be with me forever. Jobs I thought defined me. Opportunities I was sure were "God's will." All of it was removed, not as punishment, but as protection. God was making room for what He was about to bring.

The Separating Season isolated me in ways that felt unbearable. People stopped calling. Community disappeared. Even the church—the place I thought would be my refuge—became a source of pain. But in that isolation, I learned to hear God's voice clearly. I learned that His presence is enough, even when everyone else walks away.

The Preparing Season tested everything in me. My faith. My endurance. My obedience. Right now, as I write these final words, I'm still in this season. No job since August 2025. Bills unpaid. Rent overdue. Debt piling up. Yet I'm writing this book. Working on my recording project. Preparing for ministry. Because God told me to focus on what He's called me to do, not what makes sense financially. And I'm trusting Him, even when it looks foolish.

The Releasing Season is coming. I can feel it. Like when you're in winter and you start to smell spring in the air. The shift is near. The doors are about to open. The breakthrough I've been praying for, fasting for, crying for—it's coming.

And when it does, I'll be ready. Not because I'm perfect, but because I've been through the fire and came out refined.

WHAT GOD TAUGHT ME IN THE WILDERNESS

The wilderness wasn't meant to destroy me. It was meant to prepare me.

In the wilderness, I learned:

God's silence doesn't mean His absence. There were long stretches when I prayed and heard nothing. When I cried out, the heavens seemed closed. But He was there. Working behind the scenes. Orchestrating things I couldn't see. Teaching me to walk by faith, not by feeling.

Obedience unlocks the next level. Every time I delayed obeying God, my season stretched longer. But the moment I surrendered—even when it was hard, even when it didn't make sense—things shifted. Doors opened. Provision came. Peace returned.

Provision doesn't always look like abundance. Sometimes, it looks like just enough, given at exactly the right time. God didn't give me excess, but He gave me what I needed when I needed it. And that taught me to depend on Him daily rather than hoarding or trying to figure it out on my own.

The enemy attacks transitions. The closer I got to breakthrough, the harder the attacks came. The robbery. The visa denial. The attack with the iron. The spiritual warfare on my sight. All of it happened when I was about to cross over into something new. That's not coincidence. That's strategy. And recognizing it helped me stand firm instead of turning back.

Pain has purpose. Every wound I received, every tear I cried, every moment I wanted to give up—none of it was wasted. God is turning all of it into testimony. All of it into ministry. All of it into a message that will set others free.

2 Corinthians 1:4 says, *"[God] comforts us in all our troubles, so that we can comfort those in any trouble with the comfort we ourselves receive from God."*

That's why I went through what I went through. So I could comfort you. So I could tell you that if God brought me through, He'll bring you through too.

WHERE I AM NOW

As I write this conclusion, I'm in a season of transition. I'm standing on the edge of Preparing and Releasing.

I don't have it all figured out. I don't have financial security. I don't have all the answers about what comes next.

But I have faith. Faith that the God who kept me on the bathroom floor will keep me now. Faith that the God who saved me from the robbery will open doors no man can shut. Faith that the God who provided two jobs when I was homeless will provide everything I need for this next season.

This book you're holding? It's proof that God is faithful. It's proof that obedience, even when it costs you everything, is worth it.

The project I'm recording? It's coming. The ministry I'm stepping into? It's launching. The calling I've been running from, wrestling with, finally surrendering to? It's here.

And I'm ready. Scared, yes. Uncertain about the details, yes. But ready. Because I didn't survive everything I survived just to play small. I didn't break generational curses just to live a mediocre life. I was not anointed to just sit and do nothing. I didn't cross over under fire just to settle for comfort.

God didn't bring me this far to leave me. And He didn't bring you this far to leave you, either.

A WORD TO YOU

If you're reading this, it's not by accident.

Maybe you're in your own Removing season, and it feels like everything is falling apart. **Hold on.** God is making room for what He's about to bring.

Maybe you're in your Separating season, and the isolation is crushing. **Hold on.** God is speaking to you in the silence. Listen closely.

Maybe you're in your Preparing season, and it feels like the fire will never end. **Hold on.** You're being refined for something greater than you can imagine.

Maybe you're in your Releasing season, and fear is trying to hold you back. **Step out.** God has already prepared the way. Walk boldly into what He's called you to do.

Wherever you are, whatever season you're in, know this: **your pain has purpose. Your struggle has meaning. Your story matters.**

The world needs your testimony. The Kingdom needs your obedience. The next generation needs you to break the cycles so they don't have to fight the same battles.

Don't give up. Don't turn back. Don't let the enemy convince you that you've come too far to fail now.

You haven't. You're exactly where you're supposed to be. And your breakthrough is closer than you think.

THE PROMISE I'M HOLDING ONTO

Galatians 6:9 says, *"Let us not become weary in doing good, for at the proper time we will reap a harvest if we do not give up."*

"At the proper time." Not my time. Not when it's convenient. Not when it makes sense. But at God's appointed time.

I'm holding onto that promise. I'm declaring it over my life. Over my finances. Over my calling. Over everything God has spoken to me.

The harvest is coming. The release is coming. The fulfillment of every promise God made to me in the darkest seasons is coming.

And I will not give up before I see it.

Neither should you.

WHAT COMES NEXT

You might be wondering: What happens next for Dwayne? Does he get the job? Does the rent get paid? Did he get back a car? Does the ministry take off?

I don't fully know yet. What I do know is this: **God is faithful. And whatever comes next, He'll be in it.**

I know the book is done. You're holding the proof.

I know the projects are coming. The prayers are being recorded. The other ventures are coming.

I know the ministry is launching. The preaching is starting. The calling is being walked out.

I know the generational curses are broken. My children won't fight the battles I fought. My family line has been redeemed.

I know my testimony is powerful. And it's going to set people free.

But there's more. So much more. Things I can't talk about yet. Things I'm still processing. Things God is whispering that both terrify and exhilarate me.

THE FINAL WORD

If this book unsettled you, that was intentional.

Don't close it and return to your life unchanged.

Some things are meant to follow you.

Pay attention to the season you're in—

especially the one you've been avoiding.

God doesn't expose without intention, and He doesn't press without purpose.

Look at your family line.

Not the stories you tell publicly—the patterns you whisper about.

Stand where no one before you stood.

End what everyone else learned to live with.

Release the people who broke you.

Not because they're safe.

Not because they deserve peace.

But because carrying them any further will destroy you.

Answer the call anyway.

When obedience feels reckless.

When faith feels expensive.

When saying yes feels like losing something you can't replace.

Trust God's timing.
Even when heaven is silent.
Even when prayer feels unanswered.
Even when waiting starts to feel like punishment.
Especially then.
This isn't the end of the story.
It's the edge of it.
There is a chapter I can't write yet.
Not because it hasn't happened—
but because I'm still standing inside it.
God told me the test isn't over.
There is one final act of obedience He's asking of me.
Something darker than the bathroom floor.
Heavier than the beatings.
More terrifying than the robbery.
He's asking for the one thing I protected.
The one thing I justified keeping.
The one thing I told myself was off-limits.
He's asking me to place it on the altar.
And I don't know what will happen if I do.
So this is where the story stops.
Not because it's finished—
but because the decision hasn't been made.
What comes next will cost more than survival ever did.

To Be Continued...

SEASONS OF STRIPPING

Everything that came before this page had a testimony.
A story that had already been told.
A trial that had already been survived.
A God who had already shown up.
What follows is different.
This is the chapter still being written.
The season without a resolution.
The storm from the inside.
Turn the page—if you dare.

APPENDIX

A PRACTICAL GUIDE TO SPIRITUAL WARFARE

This is not a message of emotion.

It is a message of divine instruction.

Every season in this book—the stripping, the silence, the waiting, the testing—required a response that went beyond feelings. Feelings change. Circumstances shift. But spiritual strategy, rooted in obedience and faith, holds when everything else is moving.

The principles below are what I have learned through the fire. They are not theory. They are the practices that kept me standing—through the bathroom floor, the court dates, the immigration clock, the morning walks in the cold when I had no idea what was coming next.

Use them. Return to them. Share them with anyone in your life who is in a season they don't have words for yet.

FOUNDATIONAL PRINCIPLES

PRAY IN POSITION — NOT IN EMOTION

When you pray, you do not need to beg. Pray in authority—knowing who God is and what He has already given you. You are not a beggar approaching a distant king. You are a child speaking to a Father who has already heard you. Following God is not about feelings or emotions—it is a lifestyle executed daily, in faith, regardless of what you feel.

REPENTANCE ACCELERATES THE PROCESS

We cannot demand justice from God when we have violated the promises we made to Him. He is patient—but He is also just. Repentance is not weakness. It is a powerful vindicator that removes the breach between you and God, and speeds up what you have been asking for. If something feels stuck, start there.

LET GO SO GOD CAN MOVE

God cannot fully mold you into who He wants you to be until you release what He is trying to remove. He will not move until you make a choice. When your atmosphere is polluted—by the wrong people, wrong habits, and wrong agreements—you cannot grow into your destiny. Make the choice. God responds to decisions.

MOVEMENT IS PROPHETIC

If God is speaking to your heart about a goal or dream, take action—even a small action. Look at the apartment. Look at the car. Look at your credit score and how far you want it to go. Looking aligns your heart to the manifestation. It produces motivation, drive, and the kind of expectation that invites God to move. Non-movement has no miraculous results. Miracles happen when action meets activation.

GUARD YOUR MOUTH

There will be seasons when God works specifically on your tongue—because He needs your mouth to carry power, and you cannot use the same mouth to gossip and think that same mouth will defeat the enemy. Ask God for a fresh anointing on your lips. Speak what He has spoken. Let your words align with the future He is building, not the circumstances you are standing in.

SLOW EXITS STICK

When God tells you to leave something—a relationship, a habit, a season—do not exit abruptly. Abrupt exits lead to returns. Exit slowly, intentionally, with God's grace sustaining you through the process. Deliverance takes time. Give it the time it needs.

YOU CANNOT MARRY YOUR FUTURE IF YOU ARE STILL MARRIED TO YOUR PAST

There comes a moment when you stop questioning and simply obey. Some seasons, God will take you through in complete silence—you will not be able to explain to anyone what He is doing with you. That is by design. Trust the silence. Keep walking. The explanation comes on the other side.

WARFARE REFERENCE GUIDE

When you don't know what to do—start here.

Situation	Divine Responses
3-Day Fasting + Watch Hours	
Rise at 12 a.m. · 3 a.m. · 6 a.m. — Pray, Declare, Fast	
Spiritual Warfare	Begin a 3-day fast. Pray at the watch hours: 12 a.m., 3 a.m., and 6 a.m.. Declare God's authority over your life and every attack against it, and altar that has your name on it.
Laziness, no energy, no motivation, constant distraction	Change your posture. If you're sitting—stand up. If you're standing—raise your hands to the Father. Movement is prophetic. The body follows the spirit. Go to a different location, switch things up, cut some people off if you need, but most importantly: lock in.
When You Can't Hear God	Read the Word. Pray. Then wait for an answer. God is not silent—our reception is sometimes blocked. Silence is not absence.
When Prayers Go Unanswered	Ask God for forgiveness—for yourself and your family. If you have not forgiven someone, do that now. Unforgiveness can block the flow of answered prayer.
Questioning Your Calling	Close your door. Shut yourself in. Be patient. Trust. Take action in faith. Ask God to open your ears to hear Him, your eyes to get a glimpse of where He is trying to take you. Trust your spirit. Every trial is a curriculum for the assignment ahead. He has been planting you, not burying you. But all He wants is for you to spend time with Him and ask.
Running Low on Hope	Remind yourself of the promises God has made to you—not what your circumstances say, but what His Word says. Read it aloud. Let it land again.

Situation	Divine Responses
A New Level of Growth	You'll recognize spiritual growth not by perfection, but by change within you. Your prayers begin to sound different, your words carry more intention, and something shifts in how you think and respond. A quiet lightness and peace start to settle over your mind. That is the sign of transformation taking place. You are not who you were—you are stepping into a deeper level of growth. Now is the time to walk into the spaces God has already prepared for you.
Feeling stuck	Open your heart to what God wants to do in your life. Ask Him to show you what you are holding onto that He is trying to remove. Then let it go. Because the enemy will use your weakness to keep you bound, hence delaying you from your assignment. When he does not want you to move, he ties your hands from being productive. When he wants to shut your destiny down, he will shut your mouth. NEVER keep your mouth closed. Cry out. That will shift you from a place of feeling stuck to a place of purpose.
Struggling Financially	Grab your wallet. Place your hand on it and declare: "I will have an increase. I will possess and own everything that is mine. I come against every spirit of lack that comes to take what belongs to me—in Jesus' name." For the rest of the week, declare, "Ownership is mine."
Want Spiritual Growth but Feel Stuck in Sin	The enemy will try to pollute or taint your anointing, but he cannot cancel your assignment. Repent. Ask God to redevelop your sound, because the more we cry out to Him, the more he makes us like Him. Give yourself grace, because we are not perfect beings, but rather striving to become like our king, and this takes daily surrender.

Situation	Divine Responses
Repeating Patterns	It is important to notice these cycles. When you identify these patterns, it becomes easier for you to notice when they repeat, and you can prevent the next cycle from beginning by being ahead.
Waiting on God to Move	Ask yourself: Have I made a choice? God will not move until we do. Make the choice. Take one step in the direction He pointed. Movement is prophetic—it signals to heaven that you believe what you declared.
Holding On to the Vision	Look at it. Take a literal look at the car, the apartment, the credit score, the business. Looking aligns your heart to the manifestation. It gives you drive. It keeps the vision alive until the provision arrives.

This is not a formula. It is a starting place.

God is not a system to be managed—He is a Father to be known. These practices are not magic; they are the postures of a person who has decided to take God seriously. They are what I came back to every time the season got harder than I thought I could bear.

Whatever you are facing right now—bring it to Him. Not polished. Not resolved. Just honest.

He can work with honest.

You will be known as a great success and you will not be put to shame. Everyone who prays on your downfall and says you will amount to nothing, they will see you rise! Our mistakes don't define us. God does not choose you because you have never made a mistake. God chooses you because He loves you, and it doesn't matter what you've done. God will never not choose you. Because you are who He has made to impact change.

"The Lord himself goes before you and will be with you; he will never leave you nor forsake you. Do not be afraid; do not be discouraged." — Deuteronomy 31:8 (NIV)